THE GREAT DIVIDE

The Social and Cultural Context of Inequality

The Great Divide
The Social and Cultural Context of Inequality

The Great Divide
The Social and Cultural Context of Inequality

ISBN: 13:979-8635962510
IMPRINT: Indie Publishing

Printed in the United States of America
10 9 8 7 6 5 4 3 2 1

THE GREAT DIVIDE

The Social and Cultural Context of Inequality

by
Brian C. McGuire
Towson University

FAR-LEFT PUBLICATIONS

Brian C. McGuire

The Great Divide
The Social and Cultural Context of Inequality

Brian C. McGuire was born in Baltimore, Maryland on May 31, 1970. He spent thirteen years serving in the United States Armed Forces. He received a Bachelor of Science from Towson University. His areas of research interests include the mental terrain of Community Psychology: A field of Human Services that places special emphasis on problems associated with urban groups and how they adapt under low socioeconomic conditions during childhood, adolescence, and throughout the course of adult development and aging, and sociocultural influences (including theoretical concepts pertaining to how various dimensions of culture influence stress and coping).

TABLE OF CONTENTS

Dedication

This book is dedicated to anyone who has the audacity to show hope and courage in the face of overwhelming adversity. Those of you who find yourselves in a difficult or unpleasant situation from which there is no clear or easy adjustment. Might this book serve anyone who perseveres calmly despite being confronted with such distractions. Commit yourself, I say, so that your courage and tenacity might bring kindness or compassion to others. Let us move beyond our racial divisions so we may resolve genuine problems.

Acknowledgements

What we've built in this great nation of ours is a degenerate form of higher civilization. What that means is our nation's leaders are more often unrestrainedly and immorally self-indulgent. And with our government officials showing great moral corruption or wickedness, we have been divided on a great many issue. Such division describes a system in which different cultures, groups, and its members endure unequal and unfair treatment.

We are greatly divided along race, ethnicity, culture, nationality, religion, age, sexual orientation, gender, and other identity lines. For example, the great divide between Whites and Blacks or between management and workers are distinctions we regard as significant and very difficult to ignore. And as the rich get richer, what about the rest of us? The sad fact of it all is these disparities are dividing communities not just in the chocolate cities, but also in the vanilla suburbs and rural areas across this great nation of ours.

However, many people continue to remain on the humane side of the great divide. It doesn't mean succumbing to our fears or being complacent, either. Rather, it means we must confront the underlying conditions that affect our existence in America before it's too late. And, many people are doing just that. Thus, by confronting the very nature of existence in a social and cultural context, we can ensure our fight against inequality will be a victory.

I challenge you, the reader, to reexamine your basic assumptions about inequality—what does it mean and how to remove it from our existence. For me, inequality means more exploitation, oppression, and humiliation of Black, Brown, and poor people.

In my fight against inequality, I've acquired a few good friends and acquaintances, the ones who stood with me in my lowest moments and would stand with me in my greatest triumphs. Perhaps, they are an unlikely cast of individuals. But, I appreciate them none the less. These are the people I would like to acknowledge today.

I wish to express deep gratitude to Yvonne M. Drake for her love and support throughout the writing process of this book.

I am especially grateful to Anita L. Opher for her editorial genius and dedication to the development of this book.

I am deeply indebted to my magnificent son, Tevin Q. McGuire, whose creative outlook on life proved invaluable in the writing process of this book.

And finally, special thanks to Tameika Trent. Her resourcefulness in the marketing and promotion of this book has been truly a great contribution.

Prologue
On What Divides Us

It's one of the few regrets of my presidency - that the rancor and suspicion between the parties has gotten worse instead of better. There's no doubt a president with the gifts of Lincoln or Roosevelt might have better bridged the divide, and I guarantee I'll keep trying to be better so long as I hold this office.

Barrack Obama (2008 - 2016)

Well, it's 2020. And, I've missed out on ringing in the New Year. I missed out on celebrating Christmas too. I haven't been excited about celebrating Christmas since I learned about its true origin back in 1994. Christmas is a part of Teutonic Mythology. That is to say, it's a part of Viking tradition and Norse folklore. Besides, I'm no longer exited about holiday traditions tied to Europe since most are religious based and Europe never produced a religion, never!

I am excited, though, about completing the writing portion of my new book, The Great Divide: The Social and Cultural Context of Inequality. It's still early in the writing process; and, I already find myself competing against my first book, The Ignoble Paradox of Man.

It was never my intention to become an author. Researchers are only interested in publishing when they find information deemed pertinent to the community. Yet, as I sit at home, typing, I find myself holding back my eagerness to publish yet another book. It's been five long years since the publication of my first book; and, I am filled with excitement. I guess it's time to make my new findings readily available to the public.

People are forever asking me why write a second book? The publishing of a book is gratifying for many people. I've heard that statement time and again. But for me, it's not enough to know I have a well written book in global data bases around the world. I need know the book actually interest people. So, I am writing a second book just to find out if I have the firmness of character to intrigue an audience. If that takes a few more writing attempts to determine, then so be it.

My first book was a good, well written read. But, it was a bit long-winded. I haven't stopped apologizing to people about that. After five years, I find myself writing another book, not quite on racism but inequality. I received mixed reviews since I announced the idea of writing a second book. The announcements came in total silence. So, I have a lot to prove in the publication of this book. I only hope this book will prove to be of the same caliber as my first book or higher.

I try to stay away from using symbols, metaphors, and analogies in the content as this book is a straight-forward and realistic look at inequality. In the last book, I wrote about racism and racial discrimination. But I wrote the content in a paradox format. The book was symbolic from cover-to-cover. This time, there is very little symbol-ism throughout its content. Here are just a few precaution-ary measures I took to ensure there will not be a major overlap in content. The topic, artistry, the quality of literat-ure, the length of each chapter, and theme will, hopefully, appeal to a broader audience. The cover size and the amount of content share a similarity. But, that's all.

People say you can never judge a book by its cover. But, often, they do. I just hope the title and cover attracts a broader audience this time. The artistry on the first book cover was stunning up close and in person. However, I failed to use Internet friendly colors. So viewing the cover from the Internet, it lost its visual appeal to potential readers.

This book has great visual appeal. The artistry is exciting and eye-catching. And, the read is straightforward and fluent. Each chapter consists of everyday topics, nothing over the top. But, topics are uniquely defined and well written thought out. The Great Divide: The Social and Cultural Context of Inequality will prove to be a superior read to other reference books on the market.

In 2016, I watched an interesting movie called Finding Forrester, starring Sean Connery (William Forrester) and Rob Brown (Jamal). The story takes place in Manhattan. William Forrester is a reclusive writer. Jamal is a talented Black high school basketball player from the Bronx with a gift for writing. In the exposition, the protagonists meet for the first time as Jamal ends up finding Forrester.

As young prodigy and mentor, Forrester elevates Jamal's writing skills to the point of professionalism. It's at this point in time, Jamal's advancement in writing unwittingly arouses tension between himself and his new teacher. Now, pay attention to this point I make. Forrester tells Jamal a story about a man who failed in his first attempt at novel writing. He deemed himself unworthy. That man, who Forrester considered dangerous, became a teacher who tore down students he thought were better than him.

Mr. Crawford antagonized Jamal because of his potential. Forrester said Crawford's problem was he quit when he simply should've written another book. The moral of the story is you should pursue your passion with interest and enthusiasm. Quitters never win at anything. If you fail to try, truly try, you become a danger to not only yourself, but to others.

That storyline stayed with me as I transitioned from a researcher, writer, to author. My first book, though a good read, wasn't as successful as I hoped. But thanks, in part, to the movie Finding Forrester, I am in the process of writing yet a second book.

So many events happened that led to the writing of this book, I'm not sure where to begin. In the ensuing years, there were a host of topics, problems, and events that divided us. We're divided over police brutality that regressed into outright murder of Black Americans. Colin Rand Kaepernick kneeled during the National Anthem and in protest of the systemic abuse and murder of Black Americans. We're divided on whether we should continue to sing the National Anthem. Kaepernick was ostracized for having the courage and commitment to continue protesting. Sexual harassment scandals shocked a nation that was in denial. There is still the question of unequal distribution of resources. And, Americans continued to be at odds with Republicans and their choice for US Presidency.

Oh, did I mention we have an idiot and twitter junky seated in the Oval Office. Donald Trump, with his self-styled pirate approach to politics, ignited a backlash of hostility yet again but, this time, over his decision to attack Iran, also called Persia. Former President Barack Obama and his administration (2013) made small but controversial steps toward ending decades of hostilities with Iran. Trump's actions (he dismantled the Iran Nuclear deal) heightened already fragile relations with the official Islamic Republic. As the latest round of heightened tensions continued in 2020, President Donald Trump launched a missile attack at Iran's lead General for, reportedly, plotting to kill US citizens.

In 2015 President Obama, along with the powers that be, brokered a deal with Iran to end its nuclear program. That momentary lapse in peace would soon end under the Trump administration. Hostilities continued to rise in 2018 as Iran taunted the US with air strikes against US bases placed in Iraq, including the downing of a US drone. In January 2020, the US responded with a drone strike that killed at least two dozen people. Among the deceased was General Qasem Soleimani. The attack started widespread protest among Iranian citizens.

Early in 2020, we were divided over the possibility of war with Iran. The Iran controversy, like so many other wars, was about the unequal distribution of resources. Republicans backed Trump's decision to deploy military personnel to the region. Democrats were adamantly opposed to using acts of aggression before attempting peaceful negotiations. Many believed Donald Trump used the Iran controversy as a chance to gain four more years in office. Donald Trump was under possible impeachment since 2019. I didn't too much care if he was impeached. But, I anticipated a brilliant chapter on the event. Between Trump and former Mayor Catherine Pugh, chapters in this book are among the many that make for a great read.

This passage is a prologue to the complete breakdown of this book. The Great Divide: The Social and Cultural Context of Inequality is an essential read. It takes a long hard look at what the cultural elite does not want you to know. In the United States, some groups clearly have greater status, power, and wealth. These disparities are what led to the stratification of our social, economical, and political systems. This book offers a solid explanation of how the cultural elite consistently prevents Black and poor people from having access to those systems. Having access is essential for minorities and their communities to reach full equality.

Inequality is the central theme of this book. I approach it from many angles. By Design: Dumbing Down Black Americans, Black Lives Matter, and An Act of Charity: Should Blacks Receive Reparations are among the most incisive chapters on issues relevant to Black Americans. In the introduction, The Great Divide, I argue that it's always been the Oligarchy's goal to control minorities by encouraging dissent among them. In turn, I urge the country to get past its unhealthy fear of change.

Sociocultural issues are extensively discussed and intertwined throughout this book. Moreover, such issues lay the foundation for important psychological discussions and resolutions. All chapters are designed to aid readers interested in exploring how Black people cope and survive life in America. In this way, this book better prepares the reading public for the social inadequacies of contemporary society. By providing readers with important incite on problems both racial and ethnic minorities confront today, surely, The Great Divide: The Social and Cultural Context of Inequality will fit any readership looking to elevate the great debate to new intellectual and moral heights.

Far too often, a reference book is the result of scholarly research, receiving more study than it deserves. There is no systematic arrangement of scholarly order in this book. Instead, I allow the book's natural rhythm to unfold. Although most people believe a book written about inequality will be full of rhetoric or biased information, this is not the case. I work to keep daily discussions in proper sociocultural contexts. My approach to understanding sociocultural issues provide a critical perspective for analyzing and helping us understand the way we behave, think, and feel. I also believe sociocultural influences, through context, add meaning to who we are and how people interact with us in the real world.

The Great Divide: The Social and Cultural Context of Inequality serves as a harsh reminder that inequality and injustice continue to rank among society's most durable and disabling problems. Rene Descartes once said, "Divide each difficulty into as many parts as is feasible and necessary to resolve it." How fitting, as I've divided this book into many sections in order to simplify a difficult topic. Some people will continue to find it a difficult read. But, it does not require a lot of effort to read or understand. It is intended for readers who are hard to convince or persuade.

Introduction
The Great Divide

The Great Divide

Pit race against race, religion against religion, prejudice against prejudice. Divide and conquer! We must not let that happen here.

Eleanor Roosevelt (1884 – 1964)

It has always been the oligarchy's policy to maintain control over minorities by encouraging dissent among them. This divide and conquer technique is built into our social stratification system. The technique is simple. Use social, economical, and political systems to control minorities. People are granted access to structural systems according to their social classification, which is based on status. Status causes disparity among people or between groups. Thus, when "the system" fails a group, pitting one group against another, we call it the great divide. So where does that leave Americans? It leaves them divided on a great many issue.

Since 2015, we've witnessed notable deaths, acts of unspeakable cruelty, and political scandals that shocked a nation that was in denial. Law enforcement gravitated from abusing Blacks to outright murder of Black people. If that's not enough, White identity extremists or hate groups openly advocate violence on those considered inferior. And, minorities are beginning to lose their desire to assimilate into the cultural mainstream.

Meanwhile, President Donald J. Trump had more accusations levied against him, this time for allegedly violating his oath of office and using the presidency for his personal gain. And pleas for his resignation, backed by whistleblowers, and Democratic law makers, were shamefully weak and ineffective attempts to save face for a nation teetering on the brink of disaster.

On a positive note, the Baltimore Ravens had a good run this year. At one point, they were ranked as the number one football team in the league. Although, the Kansas City Chiefs won the Super bowl (2020). Colin Kaepernick's Nike sports apparel sold out of commercial stores across the nation. And, I can't help but reminisce about how Kaepernick became so famous. He stood on bended knee to protest police violence and the systemic abuse of Black Americans.

Throughout its intellectual history, America constantly failed Black people. By controlling the narrative, Kaepernick felt strongly he would uncover the truth behind America's violent past. Its past aggressions include slavery, the Eugenics movement—which was a segregation and sterilization process—and prejudice and discrimination well into the new millennium. Such unhealthy obsessions continued to disrupt the daily lives of Black people.

First term President Donald Trump took notice as Colin Rand Kaepernick attracted international attention to the plight and predicament of Blacks in America. His protest ignited Trump's fury and divided public opinion, making the great divide seem less clear and, certainly, less easy to understand. Kaepernick's goal was to raise awareness and shed light on problems effecting Blacks in America. Kneeling during the Star Spangled Banner or the National Anthem seemed a bit contrary to some folk. But the backstory and crosscurrents of it is rooted deeply in US slavery.

The National Anthem is very offensive to Black Americans. It was written in battle (1814) while America fought for its rights to preserve slavery. The racially prejudiced, downright xenophobic nature of dominant society is fueled by lyrics written in the second half of the National Anthem. Remember, many of America's early presidents were proslavery. They, in turn, helped shape this democratic experiment we call the United States of America.

The US Supreme Court is one of many American institutions that stood strongly in support of slavery. American psychiatrists, who preserved and orchestrated the eugenics movement, were responsible not only for slavery's existence, but the birth of slavery as an institution. Kaepernick—a biracial quarterback who played football for San Francisco's 49ers—was the first person to kneel when Americans stood for the National Anthem. In doing so, he showed White privilege in a clearer yet harsher context. He also exposed how racist the National Anthem was to Black people while revealing its violent past that should not be ignored. So besides the anthem, America's glorious past is devastating to Black people.

But, the Civil Rights movement (1967) should have ended undue suffrage for Blacks. Yet, dominant society continued to be in constant denial. White police abuse of authority, an unjust judicial system, and bureaucratic corruption continued to undermine laws meant to protect rights all citizens of America are supposed to possess (requisites for healthy intergroup relations). Dominant society continued to subvert these rights as conceived in US law:

> the right to vote or to receive fair treatment under the law—laws set forth in the Thirteenth, Fourteenth, and Fifteenth Amendments, the US Constitution, and in some congressional acts.

Curiously, the great abolitionist, Frederick Douglass, after reviewing the Amendments, felt none were finished or fully developed. He was fearful for the safety of Blacks and their investment as citizens in America. Even the eminent Negro scholar W. E. B. Du Bois predicted (1903) that the problem in 20th century America would be the color line. He was proven right.

Even so, the danger for Black Americans not controlling their own narrative is that dominant society gets to write a chronological account of Black people, their developments, and experiences in favor of their own triumphs. What that means is America can say whatever it wants to about Black people; and, the world would believe it.

Division of Society

Most people feel that racial divisions are a part of the American process. Since they do, most are disinterested in understanding what divides us. In the past, we regarded racial divisions as inevitable digressions of society and did not see the need to understand such things. Today, there are continued indiscretions over our racial divisions.

When there is division in society, it's from an unequal distribution of resources. One group, usually dominant society, may have more advantages over another or others. For instance, members of dominant society may live in the suburbs and rural counties where there are greater opportunities available. They also tend to have better school systems and recreational programs, which are sources of social support not readily available to people who live in city areas. Minorities tend to live in urban areas like the city. Poor housing, lack of resources, and few opportunities to advance are among the disadvantages of living in the city.

The misdistribution of resources usually occurs when society forms a social system based on class and economic status. Having status, any type of status, creates a hierarchy where some people are regarded as more important than others. Wealth, power, and income are often achieved through status. Here, the rights and needs of rich people are dealt with before or treated as more important than poor people. Thus, the great divide results from a trickle down of resources that gradually benefit the poorest as a result of increasing wealth among the richest.

The great divide can be framed in many contextual ways. But, its basic structure underlies a system of concepts that support any arguments based on right and wrong and to how people should behave. These arguments are, in effect, surrounded by traditional American moral value systems embodied in the Protestant ethic. Often angry discourse over minority improvements in society, dissenting views set the tone for expressed disagreements, conflicts, and disputes between dominant society and minorities. Such disagreements more often lead to civil action.

Claim of competition over resources among minorities for such matters as the production and consumption of goods and services (as well as the supply of money) supposedly threatens to disadvantage dominant society.

> They feel that minorities are pushing too hard too fast for upward mobility, and seeking entry into other areas of interest where they are simply unwanted. They argue that it takes time to achieve true equality and that minorities should be patient in awaiting equal status.

In institutional matters, especially under social conditions where minorities seek to gain experience, fear of immorality sets in motion the fundamental reason for disagreements. The consequence is often a micro-aggression against minorities or worst. Known as White identity extremists or, simply, White nationalists, they support false claims that leads to the systemic demise of minorities and other identity groups.

In a simple swing of the pendulum, minorities argue that the proportionate saving in costs gained by increasing levels of economic production has led to inequality for women and minorities in America. That the amount of goods or services available and the desire to acquire them, (considered as natural factors of employment), are attainable to all members of American society. They further argue that the economy is flourishing and that dominant society only claims economic hardship because many believe their status is threatened.

Further, this heated exchange over supply and demand, considered as money earned (factors regulating endurance of production), is an argument for deeper seeded issues. In addition, minorities claim that the social stratification system has demoralized minority segments by dividing members into sets based on social or economic status which has, in fact, created financial hardship for them.

The great divide is a historical problem. Minorities believe dominant society only stake their claim of disadvantage because they resent minority improvements. They also feel that the lack of political control for dominant society is an inescapable reality of global interdependence.

In contrast, dominant society believes that minorities like Black Americans disadvantaged themselves due to their lack of drive and ambition. However, many nations believe dominant society developed the social stratification system to deliberately keep Black Americans outcast, the real reason for inequality in the United States.

Integration or Separation

Members of dominant society believe America can continue to function effectively if minorities learn to live separate lives, independent of the cultural mainstream. They argue that the goal of integration may in fact encourage people to abandon their morals entirely. In contrast, some minorities feel victimization is inevitable when dominant society live their lives apart from minorities. They believe that a leopard cannot change its spots. They're troubled that sooner or later separation will increase the degree of violence.

Feelings about this issue are so strong people on one side have at times challenged certain motives and integrity of those on the other. Advocates of separation argue, voluntary withdrawal from the mainstream may be a viable method of livelihood for those who oppose integration. They further suggest that separation is a healthy adaptation of acculturation. That society can benefit from being divided into separate and distinct cultural systems.

In fact, dominant society feel minorities threaten their livelihood. They say their reasons for voting for Donald Trump was to ensure their safety and their family's place in society. They say many are tired of having to look over their shoulders to ensure their safety. There is heightening concern among them that minorities will build a degenerate form of higher civilization. The result is many members of dominant society want minorities to be teased apart from mainstream culture, especially Black people.

Dominant society believes minorities are without well defined limits or social boundaries and cannot be taught to cope or interact with members of the cultural mainstream. That Trump's decision to issue executive orders, collectively, to prevent minorities from further entry into America is the only way for them to achieve a stable, sustainable culture.

They also contend that government legislation and federal mandates on integration are more appropriate for people of European descent. And, while some minorities will likely continue to enter the country, illegally, even after witnessing family and friends' detainment, his decision works well as a deterrent for all those who may attempt to follow in their footsteps. They argue that executive orders should also be issued out to prevent Blacks from taking actions against law enforcement officers who are charged with bogus hate-crimes.

Voluntary Withdrawal
From Dominant Society

Recently, immigrants, political refugees, and other minorities contradicted previously held beliefs of dominant society. Many no longer choose to conform to a standard by which actual attainments are judged. When minority groups seek out citizenship, its members are often expected to take on the customs and cultural traits of dominant society. The hope is a few minorities will get to be united with dominant society. The process happens by first-hand contact and communication between cultural systems.

Mimicking dominant society, more often, betters their situation. In turn, minorities often imitate or mimic mainstream styles and mannerisms. Fashion, that is to say, the style in clothing, hair, and personal appearance—even their manner of walking and mental attitudes displayed through communication styles—readily reflect a people who anticipated or have a right to expect love, kindness, and friendship.

Unfortunately, we are greatly divided on the basis of race and ethnicity. When dominant society behaves in an unkind or unfriendly way toward minorities, it's more or less because of the country's unwillingness to accommodate their basic needs. In turn, many minorities feel angry and resentful. The inappropriate nature of their relationship highlights a lack of respect requisite for healthy intergroup relations. Hence, minorities begin to reject the codes and conventions of dominant society.

Today, many minorities choose to have their acclaims accredited to their own race or traditional countries. Silas Adekunle was and, perhaps still is, the highest paid robotic engineer in the world; and guess what, he's African. What a credit to his race, right? His accomplishments highlighted the valuable or useful ability of Africans. Because of Silas and others like him, people began to understand Africans had the necessary qualities required to deal with the rest of the world. Curiously, it's true most countries limit its resources from minorities until they do what is expected of them or they adopt the prevailing viewpoint. In this way, dominant society seeks to control minorities, often for their own benefit, while exploiting, oppressing, or humiliating them. Still, other countries have a hard time accommodating minorities.

The United States is said to be the most accommodating country on earth. However, due to certain religions, traditions, and social customs, it cannot accommodate every aspect of a minority's needs. Limiting the rights of minorities who come from countries that hold radical views on social, economical, or political systems has become common practice. Known as a matter of national security, certain security measures are often taken. Limiting access to government jobs and denying financial aid to certain immigrants are viewed as necessary security measures. Yet, no security measures are taken to secure the safety of minorities.

Extremists, members of dominant society, resist Muslim Americans who practice religion within American borders. Jewish synagogues also come under attack due to religious differences. Black churches burned down to the ground, their people gunned down by lone wolf terrorists, and many more die while in police custody. Why? Dominant society feels constant change is giving way to a reimagining of their country. Perhaps, at-risk is a state or condition minorities endure when America refuses to accommodate every aspect of their needs.

What We Can Do About It

What we can do about it is change. That is to say, we need to recognize that there is an unequal distribution of resources; and, it is greatly due to racial divisions. The problem is twofold. First, we need to change the homogeneous thinking strategies of America. The homo-geneous thinking strategy of Americans is downright xeno-phobic. From any onlooker's perspective, Americans appear to be all inclusive as they rally around the National Anthem to defend its patriotic message, a message particularly welcoming to people from all walks of life. For a long time, many people felt America represented all that was good, right, and just. To them, America stood as an affirmation of independence, with the exception of Republicans and their unanimous decision to vote against integration (1967).

But over the years, Americans have been consumed by conservatism. They're resistant to abrupt change in favor of preserving the status quo. Thus, for the first time ever, Americans are greatly divided over their national decree. In fact, we are coming to a point where dominant society is losing its potential to sway people to protect American values and customs out of tradition.

Black people rightfully argue racial divisions and unequal distribution of resources create disparities between identity groups in the country. The constant need to discriminate against an oppressed people readily reflects a lack of commitment to change. In this way, before we can change the thinking strategy of dominant society, America has got to get pass its unhealthy fear of minorities. Dominant society is a mean-spirited bunch filled with hate. Their ugly xenophobic resentment is the main problem source for minorities.

Secondly, the social stratification system legitimizes racial divisions. Whether individualism, paternalism, or ideological racism are inevitable digressions of society or unequal distribution of resources gradually benefits minorities and poor people, each tenet legitimizes inequality by categorizing minorities and then judging them without just cause.

Understand it is uncharacteristic of humans to be unconcerned about the next person. The problem is self-serving values like feeling good, personal distinction, and independence, have people too well-adjusted to indifference. As a people, a country, and as a nation, what divides us is indifferent to who we are as a whole. Black, White, Asian, or other, our humanity is inextricably woven into every fiber of our being. It is imbued with kindness, compassion, and understanding for others. In fact, let's move beyond our narrow-minded differences so we can resolve genuine problems.

Chapter 1
By Design: Dumbing Down Black Americans

Without education, you're not going anywhere in this world.

Malcolm X (1925 – 1965)

White liberals say they dumb down their speeches when speaking to Black people. Even British Africans like Cynthia Erivo refer to Black dialect as a bastardized tongue. Be that as it may, there might be a reason for it; and, it may very well be by design.

Doesn't it seem odd each generation appears to be less intelligent than the previous? Each generation tells the next, people were smarter in the olden days. Why? There was more social interaction, family discussions at the dinner table and, arguably, more brain stimulating activities to engage children daily. Their argument is people are tactile by nature. Thus, first-hand contact is how we learn.

Today, there is not much need for hands-on training. So, there goes learning through the sensation of touch. Technology is rapidly taking over our lives. So goes the need for social interaction. People prefer to watch television and use the Internet over reading literature, learning how to write, and listening to audios. While we develop one sensation through use of the Internet or even from playing video games, a host of other, perhaps, more important sensations are lost.

That's right! Today's children are hooked on playing video games as opposed to playing outdoors or having a simple conversation. The nuclear-family has long since been replaced by the single-family unit. How does that sound for starters? Well, older generations believe there's not much positive brain stimulation inside homes missing a parent, mainly the father figure. It sounds like signs of the times, right? However, dumbing down Black Americans—even though more of a reality then first imagined—may very well be done by design.

An American Conspiracy

Sadly, the father or male figure has been absent from the family home since the 1930's. This disturbing trend means women assumed the role of figurehead in the family household. Since the induction of social service, there have been more fathers locked out of their homes than we dare document. For instance, we witnessed the induction of public assistance programs during America's Great Depression:

> Public service agencies began a campaign to remove Black men from homes where women received public assistance. Agencies carried out this plan under the assertion that Black men were shiftless, lazy, and would not adequately provide for their family in times of need.

Here, all you need to know is before 1967, America was deeply segregated. There were White-only policies in place, which prevented minorities across the nation from attaining gainful employment:

> Unemployment meant certain rights, privileges, and economic opportunities were withheld from them, especially Black men. The absence of the male figure resulted in more poverty, increased crime, prostitut-

ion, drug abuse, and higher dropout rates in grade schools for Black and poor families. Poor housing opportunities, under-employment, unemployment, alcoholism, homelessness, and public handouts would also affect generations of Black and poor men.

The Great Depression of the 1930's signified the age of the traveling worker. Hobos, as they were called, were mainly unemployed Black men who had no prospects for work at home. Why? State and federal mandates and newly formed federal assistance programs prevented many of them from living at home. And with rumors of work in northern cities circulating down south, many decided on traveling the railways to compete for potential job prospects. The word was neighborhoods were being rebuilt in big cities to accommodate the growing population.

These newly developing neighborhoods were supposed to be America's answer to reducing urban sprawl caused by the Great Depression. Called the New Deal, it was a series of federally mandated programs, public work projects, financial reforms, and regulations enacted by President Franklin D. Roosevelt between the years 1933 and 1939. These programs were designed, specifically, to increase the economy and reduce congestion in overcrowded cities. However, programs enacted under President Roosevelt were designed to segregate American Black and poor families. Along with the steady expansion of our economic and bureaucratic systems, Black and White families were left in vastly different situations.

The New Deal was also designed to provide newly developed suburban housing to affluent White families.

Blacks and other minority families would move to urban housing projects or ghettos. What Blacks did not know was ghettos were first introduced in Venice, Italy. The Italians built ghettos in urbanized neighborhoods to segregate the Jewish community from mainstream Italy. So, when the idea resurrected in America, the plan was to use ghettos to gather together and control the migration of Black people.

The Federal Housing Administration (FHA), which was established in 1934, further segregated America by refusing to finance Whites who moved into or nearby Black neighborhoods, a policy known as redlining. Meanwhile, the FHA outsourced contracts to building contractors who would mass-produce entire communities for whites only. The only major requirements pending were no contractors could build communities for or sell homes to Black people.

Urbanized neighborhoods continued to be largely segregated. However, the Civil Rights era would bear witness to middle-class white families migrating from major cities to suburban areas. Ultimately, Blacks inherited major cities in northern areas with the help of the Jewish community. The Jewish community, made up of largely White European settlements, lived in city areas since the Great Depression.

Jews understood their oppression was not by accident but by design. They understood first-hand what segregation meant to them and Black people. But, if there were going to be a strong or sudden change in their living conditions, they would have to adapt mainstream views.

They wanted to help Black people but needed to be smart about it. What do I mean? At a time when it was unpopular to conduct business with Black people, Jews did just that. They decided that in order for them to achieve middle-class status in the United States, Jews would rent out their homes to Blacks but never sell to them. Dominant society referred to Jews as slumlords as a result. The term slumlord is a testament to how diabolical one must be to succeed in a degenerate society. And from the 1950's to 1960's, during the Civil Rights era, the White Flight movement began. Jews, along with affluent Whites, would appear in suburban and rural areas across America.

Today, Jews are a tight-knit community with social structures that include Jewish synagogues, Hebrew colleges, Jewish family associations, Jewish community centers, Jewish kin systems, and even fraternal and charitable organizations with rights to access and other privileges.

During the White Flight movement, President Dwight D. Eisenhower signed the Federal-Aid Highway Act of 1956. This interstate system served a dual purpose: first, as an integral part of America's infrastructure, it linked the country together as a whole, and second, as a military transportation system. Sometime thereafter, belt loops would be added as part of a national defense strategy.

Belt loops were added to enable military convoys to maneuver around or encircle urbanized cities. Belt loops are major roadways built around a town or city to help traffic bypass the center. The plan was to use belt loops to quarantine city residents (Black people) in the event of a national emergency, state crisis, or civil unrest. The Los Angeles riots of 1992 are classic examples.

The Los Angeles riots of 1992 occurred when four white Los Angeles police officers were acquitted in the beating of Black motorist Rodney King (1991). The US military had orders to contain the riots from spreading beyond the belt loop and into White residential communities. The military commandeered interstate highways and then surrounded areas of Los Angeles using belt loops. The riots lasted more than five days, left over fifty people dead, and more than two thousand injured. The Los Angeles riots were a first look, for many, into understanding the powers that be. For many readers, the historical account just briefed, might give you a glimpse into how "the system" was structured by design.

The feminization of Poverty

Since Black families were first dismantled by public assistance programs, single-mothers have assumed the role of figurehead or head of household. This disturbing trend means women took over financial responsibility of their children at a time when it was simply not done. Since then, there's been an increase in women who endure poverty. Called the feminization of poverty, it states that far more women than men live in poverty. Their problems often manifest through chronic living conditions. Inadequate housing, dangerous neighborhoods, burdensome responsibilities, and economic uncertainties create problems for bureaucratic systems, many now overburdened and un-responsive.

Crime is also higher in communities where single-mothers are head of households opposed to communities that have two traditional parents in the home. Low income, lack of resources, miseducation, and divorce are among the likely reasons. This disturbing trend means that far more women than men will have to support themselves and, in many cases, with one or more children. Further, women are far more likely to receive less alimony or child-support payments today than women in the past. Even when divorce settlements are delinquent, back payment is poorly enforced by the judicial system.

In unfortunate cases where women are unwedded, there is an increased chance of enduring poverty. Most unwedded childbearing women will not be married in their lifetime. The percentage of all births to unwedded childbearing women was thirty-nine percent in 2018. That means women are raising one or more children and, in many cases, without the help of the father. In these cases, many will bear two to three children over a lifespan and, often, by two or more fathers.

In nearly half of the cases involving unwedded childbearing women who marry, the divorce rate is twice the national average. That means they are twice as likely to end up supporting themselves, often, with one or more children having different fathers. Even when alimony or child-support payments are awarded to an unwedded child-bearing woman, the dollar amount settled is too low to support herself and her children.

Unwedded childbearing women are in jeopardy due to their gender identity, double jeopardy when they are Black, and triple jeopardy when unwedded and of childbearing age. Most unwedded childbearing Black women endure poverty, racism, and sexism just to highlight a few important stressors in their lives. Poverty also means many of their children will grow up enduring chronic living conditions. Many will grow up dependent on overburdened and unresponsive bureaucratic systems for financial, housing, and health assistance. Their identity, poverty, and illegitimacy will inexorably lead to a disturbing trend of threatening and uncontrollable life events such as crime and violence.

As you can tell from our discussion thus far, federal assistant programs and poverty greatly contribute to dependency among Black and poor families. Such a disturbing trend deliberately undermines the sources of social support that factor into children attaining quality education. And with the wealth and income gap increasing, this bureaucratic process we call a democracy has Black, White, and poor families greatly divided.

The Conspiracy Continues

So far, we see how government conspiracies are used as tools of oppression. We also understand how federal assistance and state mandated programs intensify and aggravate poverty, creating chronic living conditions for disadvantaged Black and poor people. In this section, we will see how and why the US Government conspired to dumb down Black society.

I can't say America has always been a democracy. Why? It was President Abraham Lincoln who jump started American Capitalism. White citizens in the north had no job prospects and were starving. The problem was southern plantation owners had all the labor they needed due to the use of slavery. So, they did not have a need to hire new labor, especially White labor. An agreement could not be reach. The Civil War ensued (1861 – 1865). And, America has been a Capitalist empire ever since.

Today, its economic and bureaucratic systems are controlled by a small community of elites we call the establishment. At one point in time, the establishment or the cultural elite controlled ninety-nine percent of the nation's wealth and most of the world capital. Today, they control trade and industrial markets and for profit rather than being controlled by state representatives.

The cultural elite, often plutocrats who inherit their wealth, seeks to control our nation for their own benefit. They often use their resources to exploit, oppress, or humiliate minority members. Case in point: At one point in time, financial aid was free for qualified students. But, after Black people began to educate themselves, the US Government required them to pay back half of their tuition. As well, the government provided federal assistance in form of financial loans. Many students were forced to take out financial loans just to cover the full cost of tuition. Paying back financial loans left many students in financial debt for years, decades even. The only other options were to attend college part-time or not at all.

Once Black people learned they could acculturate themselves through art, culture, and other manifestations of human intellectual achievement, and not necessarily through a liberal arts education, studying true sciences, or learning a vocational trade, the US Government sought to remove art programs from urban public school systems. Today, most urbanized school systems are without art and music programs. Here's my analysis on the topic, for what it's worth.

After the assassination of Dr. Martin Luther King, Jr. in 1968, the Civil Rights movement came to a halt. The government developed a strategy whereby they could prevent White people from, ever again, having to deal with a serious Black push against the powers that be. So, in 1970, the government began to deindustrialize inheritably Black cities. The deindustrialization of Black cities took away the Black man's ability to provide for his family. That was an introduction to the disintegration of the traditional Black nuclear family.

Even within the grade school system, the government removed industrial trade programs from city high schools. Art and music program came under attack, and eventually were removed. Until about 1970, Black people did not need a formal education to lead a comfortable life. Tradesmen made a decent living wage working as carpenters, masons, mechanics, or any trade belonging to that group. But, the deindustrialization of Black cities left Black families vulnerable.

Next, the government told Blacks that in order for your children to succeed, they must attend college. Tuition fees left many Black students in financial debt. Unfortunately, for about ninety-five percent of graduating college students, an advanced degree does not pay itself off as a financial investment. Vocational degrees like medicine, nursing, and science will give you a return on your investment. But, for the rest of the graduating students, they will be in debt for the remainder of their lives.

The CIA introduced crack (1980's) as a drug of choice to the inner cities of America. But, it was the Clintons who industrialized the prison complex (1990's). Countless young Black males, increasingly female, would be incarcerated in American prison systems in a spurious fight against the War on Drugs. Hundreds and thousands, even millions of young Black males were subjected to immoral treatment under the pernicious control of former President Bill Clinton. Building the prison industrial complex paved the way for the school-to-prison pipeline. Today, the prison industrial complex is a financial stock on the New York Stock Exchange. And Black people are, once again, the commodity.

Then along came Former President George Bush, Jr. He developed two initiatives: The Faith-Based Initiative and No Child Left Behind. He all but removed any chance of minority children successfully competing in the American job market simply by implementing his No Child Left Behind Act. No Child Left Behind increased illiteracy among Blacks and poor families across America. His plan was to push children through grade school, even those who were socially maladjusted or illiterate; hence, no child gets left behind.

His efforts created a disturbing national trend wherein children who were socially promoted in public schools, graduated illiterate. These children were left without the necessary skills needed to compete in the American job market. Without a proper education, having little to no vocational training, nor a sense of community, many Black children, and some young adults, would soon end up in juvenile and criminal justice systems. Called the school-to-prison pipeline, it took advantage of Black and poor families devastated by widespread illiteracy, mass unemployment, social neglect, economic abandonment, and intense police surveillance. Its policies were soon challenged.

And although the constitution forbids it, George Bush found a way to channel federal funds to Black churches. The Black church had been a staple in the lives of Black folk. All of their efforts have been undertaken by the church. Their fight against slavery, assaults by the Ku Klux Klan, segregation, and the Civil Rights struggle were all resolved through the efforts of the Black church. That's why many Black people value religion above all else.

However Bush, in buying out the church, managed to entice pastors to inform the government of any potential political activities or movements that might arise in the Black community. Financing from the faith-based initiative program is the reason why we do not see Black churches at the forefront of any post-modern liberation movements. We will not see the Black church stand up for immigration, healthcare, not even education reform. Why? The Black Church is being paid to stay out of governmental affairs.

Former President George Bush, Jr, also drove America into the worst economic recession since the Great Depression. Yet, somehow, America managed to fight what could be the longest war in US history. What was supposed to be a ten year war in Afghanistan continued well beyond its time. Meanwhile, middle-class Americans experienced a deepening crisis as many lost their homes during the national recession.

The recession caused many affluent people to move into migrant areas where they awaited government relief. Unfortunately, many never recovered. Some tried to find some level of comfort and security living in homeless encampments or tent cities. The "new homeless," as we call them, increased the poverty level, widening the great divide.

If that wasn't eventful enough, there was a new format introduced to English writing, called modern England grammar; and, it's ungrammatical. Shortly after, the government removed cursive writing from public grade school curriculums, adding to the problem of illiteracy.

A Continuing Controversy

What we're witnessing in this great nation of ours is the deliberate oversimplification of intellectual content.

Our government has simplified our daily programming in a coordinated attempt to hide unpleasant facts, especially in a political context. For example, Whitewashing greatly reduces the complication of recording history. *Whitewashing* or hiding the truth about history ensures younger generations will require more direction in life. In this way, more people learn to accept a body of doctrines as the teachings of government and society without written evidence. The reason is to prevent certain groups from succeeding in society. In this way, the government can maintain control over them. In fact, the government has deliberately oversimplified daily programming in ways that is unnatural or artificial.

Education, literature, news media, movie cinema, video games, and other mediums have become distractions in this way. These mediums interfere with concentration or take attention away from resolving problems needed to function in the real world. In fact, people are often driven to a state of great mental distress when forced to confront the daily problems of the real world.

Not many television shows today are interested in quality assurance for younger audiences, either. That means television programming can be glamorized or idealized more than it really is. Thanks to distortions in television programming, many people indulge in daydreams or fantasies to escape from everyday circumstances. Glamorizing or idealizing media makes it possible to forget about ordinary or unpleasant realities of life for a while. The problem is it often produces greater problems or difficulties instead of helping to resolve problems in the real world.

Even news media tends to romanticize entertainment or imagery in order to create sensationalism. The result is minorities are often depicted in the most lurid, shocking, and emotive ways while under discussion or investigation, especially by network media. In fact, the distortion of media imagery is so sensational that it's generally believed to be true. In this way, the oversimplification of intellectual content continues to distort reality for people.

How about removing cursive writing from educational institutions to mask the problem of illiteracy? Can you just imagine telling a PhD who signs his or her name in print that he or she is illiterate? How insulting, humiliating even! Certainly someone who cannot sign his or her name in cursive is illiterate. As for the small percentage of Americans—those who are educated at Ivy League schools and prestigious collegiate institutions—they continue to receive formal education. They advance academically and career-wise.

The conspiracy behind dumbing down Black Americans is threefold. First, it served to rebuild a menial or an unskilled labor work force. Ideally, someone has to labor in order for others to achieve wealth. As capitalists, the goal has always been for the cultural elite to amass great wealth. It was true during slavery. America was built on the exploitation of free labor. Today, America continues to capitalize or profit from unskilled labor. The premise is certain, the more laborers you have laboring, the greater your chances are of amassing wealth. So, dumbing down intellectual content like education and news media is a way to assure cheap labor for generations.

Second, it is a way for the cultural elite to restore social order. That is to say, it keeps the middle-class from meddling in its affairs. The problem was the middle-class refused to adhere to an unequal exchange of labor and resources when conducting business with Black people. The result was Black people began to amass wealth. The cultural elite or the one percenters began to lose their collective status. As the two percenters, they only controlled ninety-eight percent of America's wealth and forty-three percent of the world's capital.

As a result, the cultural elite relegated the lower middle-class to extreme levels of poverty and, for some, homelessness. By increasing homelessness, the cultural elite reduced the middle-class to a middling sort, and minimized their ability to absorb and assimilate minorities into mainstream society. Remember, assimilation bridges the gap between the larger, more dominant society and smaller, less dominant cultural groups. But wait, it doesn't end here.

The third and final step in this process was to take over and restore urbanized cities. They wanted to transform run-down and aging neighborhoods into more prosperous ones. First, they began the deportation of Black people from urban cities to independent counties.

Next, the government called for private companies to reindustrialize these cities. Their goal was to move former members of the middle-class into urban neighbor-hoods that were restored. In that way, they could change the character of a neighborhood through an influx of more affluent residents and businesses. But, it's been a struggle in both areas. That is to say, the government had minimum success enticing affluent residents to move into urbanized neighborhoods. Thus, the issue of gentrification is a continuing controversy.

What We Can Do About It

What we can do about it is recognize government conspiracies are multidimensional. First, we should acknowledge there is an established pattern of aggression present. Then there's the complicity of American racism, however subtle. Racism is indicative of your more pervasive –isms to include sexism, jingoism, and communism.

We should also recognize it reinforces common perceptions that Black people are burdening other identity groups due to their dependency in an already overburdened country. This view denies accountability for the actual history and mistreatment of Black people. The subsequent relationship between Whites and Blacks, in the grand scheme of education and business, portrays Black people as detrimental to achieving a stable economy, thus developing the false impression that Black people are the main problem source for all Americans residing in America.

Second, government conspiracies are based on White fragility or how the mere presence of Black folk tends to offend White people's fragile sensibilities. This perspective regards Black people as having no moral conscious. Amoral behavior is said to come from them existing in a primitive culture of savagery and wickedness throughout global history. Further, White people believe Black behavior continues to exist even after they were civilized though colonization in Northern and Western civilizations.

To berate a people assumes they would and should pattern themselves after the dominant society. That dominant society would have them to believe their intellectual history began with the introduction of dominant influence. So when a Black person acts out in aggression or receives a public handout—at a time when Black people offend White people's fragile sensibilities—Whites who feel especially vulnerable charge Black people with being burdensome.

Such feelings resonate well in dominant society where White people inherited poor perceptions of Black people as shiftless, lazy, and untrustworthy. These feelings are often overlooked or misunderstood to be true among Blacks too. Therefore, it's not readily recognized as potentially problematic for Black people. In stark contrast, amid their White fragility, White people conspire to oppress Black people through a political process called institutionalized discrimination.

Third, antiblack racism is their go-to on problems they cannot readily resolve in negotiations with Black people. The success of Whites in America, once thought to come from a legacy of longstanding traditions and customs that united nations, cultures, and ethnicities into a homogeneous melting pot, in actuality, is owed chiefly to their violence or aggression toward other identity groups, especially by dominating groups regularly thought to be unorganized like Black Americans.

Their social dominance, which in many cases, is most widely accepted, is viewed as the result of hard work and perseverance, grit and determination, or drive and ambition, not only by Black people but other identity groups. Many of these groups seek to reach higher social status and greater visibility in American society. Ironically, their ambitions stem from a culture of favoritism and nepotism. Such methods are regularly sought out as it can always be relied on to prevent Black people from gaining mobility without their awareness. The subtle degrees of discrimination bring satisfaction to a people who are benefiting from White privilege in America.

These three dimensions of conspiracies have a long history in America. Each one is often adopted by government members looking to oppress Blacks. Yet the recent upsurge of antiblack racism exploits two inter-dimensional characteristics of the sociopolitical landscape, which is carried out by the establishment in Washington, DC. Conservatism and xenophobia are often modeled on myths of Black perversion and immorality. In times like these, White people view Black people as hampering their efforts of achieving a utopian future. These values are generally based on social indiscretions and a longstanding history of racial violence, which increases aggression and strengthens antiblack sentiment.

On the other hand, it increases awareness among Black people while reinforcing antiblack conspiracies about their demise in America. These conspiracies feed into the denigration of Blacks at the hands of the US Government. Concern for the plight and predicament of Black people is trivialized or reduced to paranoia over a people who appear marginal simply because they cannot adapt.

Dominant society believes there can be no healthy relationships existing between the two cultural systems based on such paranoia. However, when Black concerns are taken for granted, it reduces them to people of lesser importance. And, if Black people fail to negotiate with dominant society, it further denigrates their relationship, while at the same time, establishing social dominance for Whites. In fact, their White fragility is left in tack.

For example, many White people lost their confidence after former President Barrack Obama was sworn into the Oval office. However, during Trump's presidency, there was an extreme sense of patriotism expressed among Whites, especially hostility toward minorities and other identity groups. These perceptions exist because White people felt constant change was giving way to a reimagining of their country. Under the Trump administration, Black voices were left unheard and their struggles ignored by conservative and xenophobic people alike. Conspiracies are not born from politics but by those who believe the very presence of Black people offend their sensibilities.

My argument is the US Government conspires to oppress Black people and for exploitation. Conspiracies, along with various social phobias like xenophobia, conservatism, and patriarchal prejudice, create a need to have separate and distinct cultural systems. In the process, it does exactly what the establishment wants them to do, which is give them power over the poor and vulnerable. Without access to status, power, and wealth, disparities will continue to widen the divide between identity groups. Without strong resistance against conservatism, the will to rebuild Black communities will no longer exist and the desire to preserve inner-cities will be lost.

Chapter 2
PART I
The Problem with American Leadership

Faith is the first factor in a life devoted to service. Without it, nothing is possible. With it, nothing is impossible.

Mary McLeod Bethune (1875 – 1955)

Since 1993, I have taken a long hard look at America. Its healthy curiosity with racial equality tells the world we are a democracy. But, what I find to be most troubling about this great nation of ours is its natural discomfort, uneasiness, and unhealthy fear of change.

On the one hand, America is responsible for liberating countless countries, forging unbreakable unions, and granting equal rights to everyone. Yet, on the other hand, its unhealthy preoccupation with healthcare, immigration, and public education reform shows America is ill equipped or, perhaps, unwilling to accommodate the most basic human needs. Along with a lack of national recovery efforts, I feel embarrassed or ill at ease, to say the least, we are failing as a nation.

It's not hard to understand we are failing as a nation. Crime is at an all time high. Education success is at an all time low. The mass incarceration rate for Black and Hispanic men (increasingly women) exceeds the national average. In fact, we have more Black men incarcerated today than during the high point of US slavery. Political corruption is taking its toll on our nation. I fear the problem lies not in the ill will of US citizens, but American leadership.

Might we blame Black politicians for their role in the crime and corruption witnessed in the Black community? Not one person should have to emphasize how long the Black community has seen its fair share of corruption. Unfortunately, the United States has a long history of abusing its relative power over minorities. Thus, it would be highly unacceptable for me, irresponsible even, to blame them without, at the same time, condemning the corrupt bureaucratic system that governs each and every one of us.

First, we should conduct a biographical sketch of America's bureaucratic system. Such an examination should allow us to take a long hard look at the quality of leadership that exists in this country and the bureaucracy that governs it. Second, we need to ascertain why the quantity of leadership has not been followed by a steady rise in quality leadership.

Third, we need to compare the political leaders of yesterday to the political leaders of today. Here we will gain a better understand of why today's political leaders are ill-equipped to lead our nation. Last, we will also ascertain some level of understanding why our most gifted intellectuals will not, should not or, perhaps, cannot assume the responsibility of leading our nation, and at a time when we are on the verge of a national crisis. By the end of this chapter, the truth should loom large in the minds of many.

A Biographical Sketch
Of America's Bureaucracy

In the new millennium, the bipartisanship behind American politics readily reflects the duality of past bureaucracies. President Andrew Jackson sought to advance the rights of the common man to preserve the Union against a corrupt aristocracy. When Andrew Jackson created America's bureaucratic system, only White male inheritance was recognized. Before then, the only concession made for Black people was the Three-Fifths Compromise.

The compromise—proposed by delegate James Wilson, seconded by Charles Pinckney—was a solution that would count three out of every five slaves as human when determining a state's total population. It was created for the purpose of legislative and taxation representation. Remember, Andrew Jackson, George Washington, and many early Presidents were proslavery. Since America refused to recognize its' deeply discriminatory past, the old-fashioned, White-only policies of yesterday's bureau-cracy remains strong.

The Problem with
American Political
Leadership

Make no mistake about it! America's bureaucratic system affects each and every one of us. It has complex rules and regulations, which are supposed to be applied rigidly. But it's left up to interpretation, which is why minorities regard the system as oppressive. It has an established social order with some members regarded as more important than others. Unfortunately, that pecking order has unhealthy social effects not only on our nation's leaders but also the cultural elite, many of whom venture into politics.

American bureaucracy has adverse reactions on our nation's leaders. Its unhealthy and unwelcomed social effects create conflict between their genuinely egalitarian values and their own negative feelings toward minorities. Such ambivalence causes them to experience discomfort, uneasiness, and fear of change. These symptoms develop from their unhealthy fear of admixing with minorities. Why? Admixing might jeopardize their place or status in society.

Aversion more often manifests in the policies and laws they create, laws minorities find oppressive. Pretentious, right? One requisite for being a politician is an unfettered commitment to untruth. To live one's life as a lie is to be exempted from worrying about problems that affect minorities. Second, one must more or less be distant from learning how life works in the real world. There is usually a strong sense of entitlement and exemption that accompanies the individual's attitude. In fact, it's expected! Therefore, political leadership is a question of quantity as it has yet to be followed by a rise in quality leadership.

Some people say our nation's leaders are out of touch with important constitutional changes in society. Why? Many political leaders are affluent and far removed from problems of the real world. Others believe our nation is in deep crisis. Why? Many of them are happy with the current state of affairs. That much is true. Still, more are highbrow and only show concern for the well-heeled.

They're sent to Harvard, Yale, and Princeton to get the best education money can buy. As a history and tradition, most are taught the manifest destiny "Go West, young man!" After college, they move out of the house to expand their territory and consume masses of land area as considered necessary, perhaps, for survival. As a result, the real problem is that many of our nation's leaders have never been in touch with the real world. And so, they are not effective enough to lead our nation.

Many of our nation's leaders show no concern for minorities. They're taught to put personal concerns and interests ahead of others. They obtain personal goals like feeling good, personal distinction, and independence. Why? Self-serving values are useful or suitable due to its convenience, making life easier, or not involving much trouble or effort. Thus, any reason a politician gives for entering into politics should not be rejoiced or celebrated, but cautiously approached.

Self-serving values cause social phobias like aversion, xenophobia, nihilism, and conservatism. As a result, politicians will serve themselves by attaining high profile careers that benefit only them or a select few. As a consequence, many leaders have little understanding or show no concern for the daily problems affecting minorities. For them, there is no concern for moral commit-ment to community or wellness, only personal accomplish-ments and attainments. For those reasons, many of our nation's leaders are not worthy to lead. Therefore, there has yet to be an upsurge of competent political leaders.

Today's politicians are self-serving, affluent professionals who really want a large White constituency. Yet, they need a loyal minority following to succeed in winning public trust. You know the ones! We hear from them every four years during election; they then appear on television programming engaged in political commentary; and, they befriend you while on the campaign trail to elicit important minority votes.

But, we never see them engage the community, take part in open protest, or advocate for social change. Whenever they do, it's always empty rhetoric. And why is that? Many say they feel more comfortable putting their energies where best served. When in actuality, they're more comfortable not rocking the proverbial boat or hastily being stoic. And while many may be heartfelt about resolving important problems, they never take the time or have the ability to act.

Many politicians—young, willing, able—have a strong desire to succeed and are more than eager to learn. They appear to understand there is a great deal of work ahead. But, they lack the ability to understand or show concern for certain consequences. When new politicians take political office, they're often told to be seen and not heard. At other times, they're told to learn how the political system works before taking on a lead role. Disguised as mentors, senor politicians (among them our nation's leaders) often manipulate the freshman class for the purpose of preserving the status quo, maintaining traditional values, or working against instigating change in public policy. For many new politicians, buying into the worst aspects of a political system is merely a matter of profession.

New politicians often model themselves after our nation's leaders. Modeling ensures they learn the best approach to politics. We even see them out on the campaign trail, eliciting public support. Unfortunately, it's usually with limited knowledge and/or concern for consequences. Donald Trump's campaign slogan, Make American Great Again (MAGA), was modeled after Ronald Reagan's catchphrase he coined during his presidential campaign. Even Trump's bait-and-switch approach to improving the economy was a modeling of classic Reaganomics.

His mishandling of US-Ukrainian affairs was a direct result of his limited knowledge and/or concern for consequences. His impeachment hearings took place as a direct consequence of that negligence. If ever you wondered why politicians appeared to advocate for the working class while campaigning, and then become complete critics once appointed to office, it's usually because of modeling. For others—those who learn the pros and cons of politics—they deal with impropriety (inappropriate behavior or undesirable political beliefs) by turning a blind eye.

Many politicians learn to ignore undesirable political beliefs. They seem to understand the menace behind bureaucratic corruption and pay no attention. Instead, they concentrate their efforts where they can best serve the public. These politicians show admirable patience and endurance during adversity. Stoic, these wise monkeys of politics see no evil, hear no evil, and speak no evil as they learn about its advantages and disadvantages. But what many fail to understand is the learning of a process without truly understanding how it works is a case of monkey see, monkey do. Or, dare I say, monkey see, monkey do nothing.

Case in point: Congressman Elijah E. Cummings served in the United States House of Representatives for Maryland's 7th congressional district from 1996 until his death in 2019. What many people fail to understand about this political leader is he developed many of his views from Malcolm X. Coming from humble beginnings, Congressman Cummings understood the sometimes painful education people endure from life's tender circumstances.

As a Civil Rights champion, he was very outspoken. Therefore, he expressed many of his political views directly, frankly, fiercely, and in the face of overwhelming adversity. He also headed one of the US House committees, leading an impeachment inquiry into Donald Trump. Yet, he was stoic on a few occasions.

He was always implicit about his promises to the City of Baltimore, but never provided real services to its residents. Baltimore is a city that tore itself apart after the assassination of Dr. Martin Luther King, Jr. (1968). The city existed as a slum ever since. Yet, as the highest profiled politician in Congress, Elijah Cummings was all but quiet when it came down to the restoration of his city.

Congressman Cummings was also the contact person for military personnel seeking advice outside the military chain of command. Yet he refused to help military personnel to get their affairs in order, any personnel who were at odds with the United States Special Operations Command. Cummings may have been a high profile politician. But, he too endured adversity. In short, there is a real or an imagined pressure to conform in American politics.

Indeed, there are those who wanted to preserve the status quo. Others worked to protect private interests. Still, a few say they work to restore public trust in a failing system. Yes, it's all true! But the problem is, once in office, most politicians are not available to the general public. In this way, the quality of politicians remains low.

Times are exciting, though! On the rise is a group of newcomers. They're an extraordinary class of freshman congresswomen. They have a quality in them shaped and colored by their eagerness to confront the establishment in Washington, DC. They advocate for change, not only in politics, but public policy. Known on Capitol Hill as "the Squad," they are current champions of human rights.

US Representatives Alexandria Ocasio-Cortez, Ilhan Omar, Ayanna Pressley, and Rashida Tlaib were elected to the United States House of Representatives during the 2018 US elections. A small democratic group of minority women, the Squad, wants to ensure all people who land on these great shores in search of freedom have unalienable rights. By taking on immigration, healthcare, and education reform, they share a common commitment to grassroots politics. They are unabashed by criticism. They shocked America by traumatizing Republicans, thrilling progressives, and reinvigorating Democrats. President Donald Trump made racist accusations toward "the Squad." He told each member to go back to her former country and take care of the problems there.

Each member of "the Squad" is a United States citizen. Bringing a new energy and tireless passion to service, they are the new motivations of our time. They carry the torch for women of extraordinary circumstances—amazing women like Susan B. Anthony, Shirley Anita Saint Hill Chisholm, Barbara Charline Jordan, and Mary Jane McLeod Bethune—and others who came before in pursuit of true freedom. The white dress outfits worn by "the Squad" and other women members of congress during the 2018 US State of Address was a powerful display of women solidarity. That evening, they recognized the voting power of working class women. Susan B. Anthony and other women martyrs of the early 20th century wore white to recognize their rights to vote. Their deep commitment showed they were a serious force to take into account.

Ocasio-Cortez, Omar, Pressley, and Tlaib are notably angry at the current bureaucratic system and genuinely concerned about the wellness of ordinary, working class citizens. Yet, it's the conservative types like Mike Pence who continue to dominate politics. Politicians like Pence lack genuine authenticity and show no display of humility. What stands out about "the Squad" is their genuine concern for everyday, ordinary people. Whenever one hears or see them speak, you get the feeling that there is a legitimate sense of urgency that's in need of address. You're even put under the belief that life as we know it will cease to exist under the current system or get better under their administration.

In stark contrast, most political leaders today are emotionally absent when it comes to the working class. They're too concerned about exploiting their success to instigate social change. Even when they make an appeal to the public, their display is more performance than heartfelt and more rhetorical than genuine. Ocasio-Cortez, Omar, Pressley, and Tlaib are emboldened by their compassion and genuine concern for people whereas other politicians are courageous about saving their own careers.

Most nearly, "the Squad" is an example of change. Yes change, especially Omar "the Muslim" who has come under constant attack by dominant society for her style of dress. She is a nonconformist who dominant society fears. In this way:

> Its members fear the same exclusionary policy of racial inequality they imposed on minorities through-out their intellectual history.

Today's changing demographic tapestry reflects a society in which people are apparently working to correct such cultural discrepancies. Corrections are being made even though conservatives continue to resist change. That conservative people fear change often plays an enormous role in whether dominant society will become more sensitive to the daily hassles of minorities. Or, is it possible they will become listless and inactive in their resistance toward further change.

Noted: Many people will frown with mocked disapproval over any negative comments made about our nation's leaders. However, we need to point out a few differences between today's politicians and the politicians of the Civil Rights era. Try to understand any seemingly unfair comparisons made in this book serve only to enlighten the public of their differences. Now, let's take a look at Shirley Anita Saint Hill Chisholm.

Shirley Chisholm was the first African American woman elected to Congress. She developed enthusiasm for politics in college. After teaching, she successfully ran for US Congress. Shirley Chisholm was a nonconformist or a political Maverick. Her seemingly outspoken nature cost Chisholm the presidency (1972). She also protested in order to preserve social programs that suffered as a result of the establishment. Shirley Chisholm was a catalyst for change in America.

What people best remember about Shirley Chisholm was her keen speeches on Civil Rights. She had an earnest yet demanding quality to her speeches. In fact, her speeches were important or grave enough to require careful thought and attention. Chisholm's speeches were so keen, she convinced people they were truly in the fight of their lives. They also believed her combative nature motivated her fiery, passionate personality.

In a similar vein, Kamala Harris left law to enter politics (2017). Today, she is one of our nation's leaders as the junior United States Senator from California. Harris came to the Senate shrewd and knowledgeable of politics. She rose to political success by visiting with, developing resources for, and making personal commitments to various politicians and diplomats. Yet during her presidential candidacy, she was the somewhat less unpleasant in comparison to a few other poor choices.

Unfortunately, she made another unlikely electoral candidate appear as the only viable choice. Harris advocated for policies that left many people under the false impression that following the establishment was the only way to progress. After learning of Kamala Harris, people got the sense she was the lesser of two evils. Her political speeches were good. But, she was arrogant and lacked a genuine feeling for the issues. The one thing people failed to get from her discussions was a general sense of trust. Kamala Harris dropped out of the presidential race after losing important endorsements.

Kamala Harris was left challenged after a 2020 political debate with Tulsi Gabbard. After Harris and Gabbard clashed on the debate stage, Harris ended her campaign for president. But, she was always fraught with problems, problems that would weaken her performance as a presidential candidate. Due to attachment issues with her father, Kamala Harris manifested a distrust of Black men. Or so it seems. People say it became apparent in who she chose to marry. It also became evident in her arrest record as state prosecutor and state attorney general.

She imprisoned over fifteen hundred people for marijuana use. An overwhelming majority were Black.

These crimes, in the state of California, are viewed as otherwise less offensive to the judicial process. She blocked evidence that would free an innocent Black man (Kevin Cooper) from death row until the New York Times exposed her, forcing her to comply. She kept people in prison beyond their sentences to use them as cheep labor for California. And, she fought to keep tax bail systems in place that negatively impacted poor people.

Borrowing a comparison from Cornel West, we can measure three archetypes against today's political leaders: the race-effacing managerial leader, the race-identifying protest leader, and the race-transcending prophetic leader. The first archetype is the embodiment of the race-effacing managerial leader. This political leader is interested in building a large majority voter following while keeping a loyal minority base.

His or her career is built on sheer political savvy owing much success to personal skill and wit. But, do not look for him or her to be the people's choice as this politician is the better of two unattractive choices. This political leader claims to be an agent of change but works to preserve the status quo. Kamala Harris is a classic example of the race-effacing, managerial leader.

The second archetype is the race-identifying protest leader who has supposed connections to minorities. A lot of the political rhetoric used to attract an audience is in the tradition of great minority leaders like Susan B. Anthony, Shirley Anita Saint Hill Chisholm, Barbara Charline Jordan, and Mary Jane McLeod Bethune. Yet, the identity and life course perspective of this politician signifies the intellectual experiences of a person who has deluded feelings of supremacy.

Ironically, as a majority, he or she works more in the tradition of John F. Kennedy. Kennedy found his footing with Black folks during the Civil Rights era. As a political leader, the person will assert his or her power by brokering between dominant society and minorities to ensure stability among minority groups.

As a leader of minorities, the politician functions like a Shirley Chisholm. This person works to affect the distribution of political or economic power by exerting influence with the cultural elite. This person limits himself or herself by working to strengthen relations between two cultural systems and not the masses. Remember, Shirley Chisholm lost the presidential elections (1972) due to her passion to protect the best interests of women and Blacks. As a result, Chisholm's personality wasn't received well with many of her party members. Al Sharpton and Minister Louis Farrakhan are passionate leaders who do not mesh with members of mainstream culture, much like Shirley Chisholm. Due to their commitment to the Black community and not the masses, both are examples of the race-identifying protest leader.

Last is the race-transcending prophetic leader. This leadership type may be on the rise in contemporary 21st century America. The Squad is one group that appealed to the masses by crossing racial boundaries. And, they did not let discrimination stop them. Each existing member has that special quality needed to transcend races across all cultures.

Each member is politically savvy yet highly moral, courageous, and patient. But, the one thing they are not is stoic. In fact, they are outspoken, assertive, honest, and highly professional. Attributes we have yet to see in recent leaders. The Squad might just close that empty feeling of hopelessness that has consumed the American people. Bernie Sanders is another person who is on his way to becoming a race-transcending profit leader. He may someday succeed! The one thing these politicians do not consider is buying into the current bureaucratic system.

What We Can Do About It

What we can do about it is recognize that the problem with political leadership is inseparable from yet identical to the prevailing current of thought. The problem is threefold. First, we need to understand our bureaucracy is a corrupt system. Much like an aristocracy, our bureaucratic system puts power into the hands of a small, privileged few.

Over the years, our bureaucracy has come to be associated with the cultural elite. These small privileged few show dishonesty by exploiting their position of power. Their dishonesty allows them to exploit the people's trust for personal gain. Suzy Kassem (2020) said "a system is corrupt when it is strictly profit-driven, [and] not driven to serve the best interests of its people." And in American society, conservative ideology exhausts any and every honest potential.

As well, many Americans are inspired by conservatism. They have a tendency to support gradual rather than abrupt change. They also have a vested interest in maintaining the status quo. Meanwhile, people in Middle America felt they were abandoned by mainstream society. Many felt they were in a critical state of national crisis. They believed the government was taking on some of the most volatile problems confronting American society to date. Yet, our nation's leaders lacked the ability to anticipate possibly unstable and potentially dangerous circumstances. So, when Donald Trump promised to bring back jobs that were outsourced to international businesses, few people could avoid being easily swayed to vote for the right-of-centered.

Black Democratic leaders rightfully underscored problems of racial discrimination, intergroup violence, and slow racial progress, which all but destroy Republicans and their chance to function progressively. Yet, although they do not appear to be preoccupied with race, moderates refusal to prioritize minorities high on their agenda highlights the resistance of grassroots organizing most important to democratic accountability.

Conservative Black Democrats also take part in our listless bureaucratic system filled with political corruption, a failing economy, lack of public trust, and a slow mediocre rise in quality leadership. Poor quality leadership comes not only from a lack of moral vision, but also from established systems whereby the rules are open to interpretation.

Second, such failing systems help prepare for and facilitate self-serving values. Public figures—whose undesirable beliefs or inappropriate behavior makes them more narrow-minded in their personal views—are filled with xenophobic resentment. Nancy Pelosi, Julia Acosta (who was a senior civil rights investigator), even Democrats like Hilary R. Clinton—who I feel dislikes Black people, feeblemindedly attempt to be progressive, or dare I say, hide their xenophobia whether their agenda is well known or not. They are supposed to fight for the civil rights of minorities, or initiate progressive strategies to make changes in public policy. Yet, these leadership types not only exclude minorities from their agendas, but make more ambiguous the idea of inclusion to strangers and others. In this way, our nation's leaders greatly contribute to an intense dislike or a fear of change, change they are supposed to embrace: the changing demographic tapestry of American culture, for example.

Third, we must rid the nation of its conservative leaders. Conservatism is problematic in both political spheres. It promotes the notion that change, specifically abrupt or radical change, will lead the nation to a more degenerate form of higher civilization. Conservatism appears to be increasing in number not only in US Government, but among members of society.

Our nation's leaders engage in extreme forms of nationalism and conservatism to keep power and control from the oppressed. Thus, they're totally apathetic to anyone who would make accommodations to minorities and their needs. Donald Trump's proven ability to bring about hatred to minorities is sheer cunnery. He has truly proven himself to be indifferent to all minorities even though he continues to elicit support from many.

However, American leadership can be eradicated simply by acknowledging it. Understand it has to be a national effort using public and political forums to discuss it. We will also have to abolish the Electoral College if America is to become a true democracy. Making decisions whereby the popular vote has no intrinsic value on a presidential nominee is unjust. It encourages the notion that ordinary people cannot, will not, nor should not make a difference in the direction our nation is shaped.

Rather, it's more about acknowledging that not only our bureaucratic system is problematic, but needing to remove political leaders from office when they are ineffectual. It would show the world that Americans are committed enough to succeed as a nation. It would also show the world that what evokes and eulogizes the history, traditions, and struggles of the American people is worth preserving. And, it's about shaping our country into a state of national consciousness.

But it can't be done without changing the homo-geneous thinking strategies of America. Diversifying America is the ultimate goal. Thus, we must first have the kind of discussions that allow us to revamp our current social systems so there can be no narrow-minded decisions left up to interpretation. It doesn't necessarily take critical and tactical thinking, but honest thinking to instigate change in politics and public policy. After all, had we honest politicians in the Electoral College, Donald Trump would have returned to business, and Ronald Reagan would have returned to acting, not politics. And, Americans would now understand why Hilary R. Clinton was unworthy as well.

Next, in part two of this chapter, we will take a look at the fundamental problem with our nation's intellectual leaders. Their courage, sacrifice, compassion, and even their short-comings await your courageous commitment.

Chapter 2
PART II
The Problem with Intellectual Leadership

It seems our political leaders are responsible for the way we perceive the world. One way to look at how their influences interact to shape our perception is the understanding all people are endowed with inalienable rights to life, liberty, and the pursuit of happiness. What that means is all citizens are protected under the Thirteenth, Fourteenth, and Fifteenth Amendments, amendments to the Constitution, which extended civil and legal protections to all citizens regardless of race, color, or creed. Next, we will discuss the problem with our intellectual leaders, their perceptions, and how it affects who we are as a people.

The Problem with
Intellectual Leadership

Gone are the intellectual leaders of yesterday. The race-transcending prophets who possessed the mental faculties of object reasoning. Yet, their lives were characterized by actions or deeds not words or intellectual matters. Instead, the intellectual leaders of yesterday are survived by intelligent responders, noteworthy intellectuals who profess their intelligence as a tradition.

Today's intellectuals take a back seat to frontline fighting against the establishment. They are locked away in universities and colleges, far removed from the daily hassles of everyday, ordinary living. They are unimpressionable and thus able to give quick written or verbal answers when considering and presenting facts. Yet, they're opportunistic toward personal goals.

These intellectuals are fine-sounding, and seem to have a special quality. Still, they are more cautious when openly talking about the state of affairs. They come from a vast array of backgrounds and offer various solutions, some abstract, others concrete. Each talks the talk as they are experts in their field and have written numerous books on the topic. Others are highly intelligent and able to quickly adapt to the rules or conventions. A few have no problems offering solutions through their writing. But for them, that's just where it ends. They fail to direct their energies at taking action. Thus, many appear insincere when they appeal their concerns to the public.

The irony is most intellectuals will not deliberately offend the establishment once they receive their certifications and credentials. Fear of ostracism is why so many intellectuals remain stoic on political matters. So, public intellectuals like Drs. Umar Johnson and Cornel West are more often viewed with contempt for talking truth to power even among their colleagues.

The first type of intelligent responder can be found at elite colleges and universities. These intellectuals are socially distant from members of their own community. Many feel like they have a good understanding of, and are better able to deal with, problems confronting minorities. Yet they only talk about community problems in the abstract.

Or, they fail to bring about proper solutions to community-based problems. In fact, they are hidden in universities, do not engage in minority issues, write pear-review papers no one reads, and do work in academia that does not help to resolve problems in minority segments of society. Others refuse to identify or interact with former members of their community, even on campus. They remove themselves from duties that morally obligate them to discuss deep, intellectual matters about problems in their communities.

As members of the academic elite, these race-distancing scholars joined a core of aspiring intellectuals. Their new status puts a premium on those who are willing to mimic the jargon of past scholars. Those who model themselves after prominent and prestigious scholars help to maintain racial hierarchies reinforced by elite collegiate institutions.

They believe their necessity for higher education brings forth better leadership, placing them among the leading ten percent of minorities. Although many people strive to solve minority problems we see happening in our society, these elitists feel only they understand how to better address societal problems concerning their people.

Unfortunately, they're unapologetic in their critique of minorities. Their ability to speak the unspoken truth about their people makes them lose favor in certain spheres. Their candor seems to warrant denigration of marginal behavior among minorities—even at times when they are attempting to commend them for being uniquely resourceful people—as if it were unfashionable to speak favorably about them.

But, the lack or loss of compassion for marginal people may reveal a deeper, internalized crisis within them.

The irony is most become marginal members of the academic elite. They find themselves responding like those who came before them just to save their careers. Still, others find certain success among prestigious colleagues through their critical analysis of minorities. I believe John Hamilton McWhorter, V, is an example.

John H. McWhorter, V, is an American linguist at the prestigious Columbia University. He compares and contrasts critical differences in languages like jargon and colloquialism, vernacular and dialect, slang and Ebonics, et cetera. His books reveal a sense of demoralization or, at least, conflict for him. He has written numerous books about Blacks with conflicting titles ranging from Losing the Race: Self-Sabotage in Black America to Winning the Race: Beyond the Crisis in Black America and from Our Magnificent Bastard Tongue to All about the Beat: Why Hip-Hop Can't Save Black America. Thus, it may be fair to say McWhorter may have opinions that bring about personal challenges concerning his people. That or he considers the prevailing school of thought problematic or, at best, a challenge.

In contrast, Michael Eric Dyson is an example of the race-embracing archetype. Eric Dyson, as he likes to be called, is one of the first public intellectuals who made himself readily available to people in the community. He recognized that there were many problems existing in his community. That one of the greatest problems existing for his people was an absence of intellectuals willing to engage them.

Now, there is no need to say, "Brian, you're falling on deaf ears" when talking about certain intellectuals. Many are the leading most authority in their field and greatly admired. Just know you're preaching to the choir. But again, try to understand that any seemingly unfair comparisons made in this book serve to enlighten the public.

Scholars like Michael Eric Dyson are high caliber intellectuals. They're also effective communicators who would make good leaders. They're seemingly fine choices to forward a cause, start a movement, or have a revolution even. They're often introduced into society as profound scholars, prophetic in tradition.

We see them in debates, at national conventions, and during summit conferences. Many identify well with their people. They also show support for the upheaval of their people. They have no problems talking about a corrupted bureaucracy, either. But their best attribute is the ability to reach an untapped audience of working class people. …sounds impressive, right?

It appears Eric Dyson, in particular, has lost his bearings. Dyson appears more concerned about how well he articulates himself than taking action. And when you hear him speak, his beliefs and values seem forced or overly clever. Recently, Dyson wanted the US Government to create an IRA or individual reparations account for White people. In the exchange, Whites would hand out cash donations to Black people they felt were deserving or in need.

For instance, White people could give higher tips to a Black waitress thought deserving. Or, a White person could give higher wages to a Black man who cuts lawns. Dyson says he's happy to hear his proposal makes people uncomfortable. He felt that if the topic fails to make you uncomfortable, it's not effective. If solving problems doesn't cost you anything, you're not engaged in change. You're engaged in convenience, he says! Be that as it may! What an act of desperation from Dyson! His reparations proposal is nothing more than an example of token exchange: a shiny new nickel followed by the symbolic head rub.

Fortunately, Blacks do not need Whites to agree with them to take a particular course of action. A reparations program should be put in place but not for the sake of charity. Martin Luther King, Jr. once said charity is a poor substitution for justice. Truly, there would be no justice served through charity, no lessons to be learned, nor responsibilities assumed. There would be no sacrifices made to recover that which was lost. It would only be people doing what's convenient for them. Eric Dyson may have fallen from grace by proposing his IRA or individual reparations plan. But, it doesn't mean he can't recover and continue to move forward.

Despite spending eight years in exile, some people believe Dr. Cornel West is a race-transcending profit. There are those who believe Former President Barack Obama has Dr. Cornel West transfixed on tearing down young intellectuals like Ta-Nehisi Coates. Coates referred to

Obama as an acumination of Malcolm X. Dr. West felt Coates, with his naïve comparison, unintentionally misrepresented what was meant by the history of the Black freedom struggle. That Coates, in his youthful indiscretions, misled an entire generation of people by pushing "a Black face of the American empire" on an unsuspecting number of generational young people. Coates' problem, as Dr. West pointed out, was his effort to negate conversations on paternalism and imperialism when discussing White supremacy.

Now, quibbling over phraseology may seem petty. But, Dr. West only spoke to reprove or advise Coates on being historically correct in his use of formal semantics. Curiously, people believed that when Barack Obama overlooked Dr. West and his potential services in the white House, Dr. West began a hate campaign against Obama and those who praised him.

Dr. West, or Cornel as he likes to be called, admitted he harbored ill feelings toward the Former President after he failed to invite Cornel to the inauguration (2009). Brother Cornel said he fell from grace. True as it may be, he was ostracized for being critical of the Former President on political matters. So, while Black people were eight years in power during the Obama administration, Cornel fell eight years from grace.

Cornel, a man of action, stepped up and became a part of a modern freedom movement in America. As a political activist, he fully embraced demonstrations and open protests for any cause deemed to be moral, right, or just. Due to his unwavering commitment to justice—and in spite of his ties to prominent and prestigious institutions of higher learning—Cornel may very well fit the bill when it comes to being a race-transcending prophet. Although Cornel had a formal education and was not self-styled, like the late great James Baldwin, he was courageous, full of integrity, and had a deep moral vision articulated in his understanding of what mattered.

What most people fail to realize is that Cornel had always been a political activist and academician. He came into prominence in the early 1990's with his book Race Matters (1993 - 1994). His achievements and titles gave him a platform to instigate social change in the thinking strategies of dominant society. His compassion for people is understood as the basis of his actions.

Cornel proved to be highly productive, resulting from a period prolific of creative achievements spanning decades before falling from grace. His remarkable recovery is a testament to his courage and skill. After all, stumbling is not a fall.

With the exception of Dr. West, the present generation has yet to produce another important public figure who captures the characteristic spirit of past intellectuals. We have neither an Ida B. Wells-Barnett nor a W. E. B. Du Bois. This void added considerable pressure on today's intellectuals, many of whom will not come forward and assume responsibility.

What We Can Do About It

What we can do about it is appeal to their sensibilities. That is to say, we need to require intellectuals to give back to their communities. Unfortunately, the United States is a nation filled with intellectuals who are more than willing to teach academics oppose to resolving real world issues or community-based problems:

> Most intellectuals say they have no time for such matters. Their only concern is with the arts or sciences.

> Others admit to having vast knowledge on the subject matter but feel they aren't cut out for the riggers and hassles of orchestrating or participating in peace marches, rallies, and open protests just for starters. That's why they write books on the topic.

> Still, more of today's intellectuals are concerned with self-preservation. They place their personal needs and wishes ahead of other people.

Sadly, the public tends to believe people are woefully out of debt when it comes to fighting against the establishment in Washington, DC. Many are under the false impression that the US Government cannot be made to do right or people have no power to change laws.

Certainly, it's not like the public and intellectual leadership are sheltered from such matters. The information is abundant, even though in the past, much of it was misinformation. Double standards in grade school text-books, in voting rights, or unequal distribution of resources greatly contributed to America's unhealthy preoccupation with inequality.

People received very little information from their parents on the topic. A large percent of the younger generation say they cannot talk freely about race matters or political protesting with their parents. Since parents so inadequately handle information on equality, it is not surprising that a majority of them prefer to let television do the job. A large majority of parents prefer not to discuss such matters at the dinner table, in home settings, nor in church, which is known for its handling of race matters and civil rights issues. Differences in opinions are perhaps why the great divide is so controversial.

Education or information, alone, may not be enough to resolve today's problems. Perhaps educating the public through public courses and seminars, especially in academic settings, may help to change our present situation. But, it would also mean our government readily accepts change and is open to the idea of equality. Either way, it appears the public is caught in a bad situation. The only viable way to handle the problem with intellectual leadership, or a lack thereof, is to appeal to their consciousness. Let intellectuals decide for themselves what's right or wrong, rather than letting the rules or laws dictate what they can or cannot do.

Chapter 3
Bureaucratic Corruption

A system is corrupt when it is strictly profit-driven, not driven
to serve the best interests of its people.

Suzy Kassem (2020)

As I sit here, trying to figure out how I should approach this chapter, an old adage comes to mind, one I first heard from my grandmother. On the subject of hypocrisy, she referred to it as the pot calling the kettle black. And as far as former Mayor Catherine E. Pugh goes, that's exactly what we had, the pot calling the kettle black. What a powerful statement my grandmother made as I sit here, thinking about how then-Mayoral candidate Catherine Pugh spoke begrudgingly about former Mayor Shelia Dixon. If you don't understand where I'm coming from on the matter, then I will explain it to you.

It's late January 2020, and I'm sitting at home trying to complete this chapter on bureaucratic corruption. The problem was former Mayor Catherine E. Pugh awaited trial for criminal charges of fraud, embezzlement, and two counts of tax invasion. So I was left with a dilemma. Should I wait to hear the results of Pugh's sentencing? Or, do I complete the chapter, and leave the results of her sentencing for you to find out. Her sentencing was scheduled for February 27, 2020. But wait, Pugh had a few new charges awaiting her, and the results would be a nice addition to this chapter.

I mean really, talking about the pot calling the kettle black. And, she was a wolf in sheep's clothing too. Ms. Pugh had the City of Baltimore fooled for a few years. It appeared many people were tricked or deceived by her promises. So, when she was said to have betrayed her oath of office, many people had trouble believing Ms. Pugh was the focus of a political scandal. It would take a few days before a feeling of despair would come to haunt the good people of Baltimore.

Desirous Of Change

In 2016, Baltimore City Mayoral candidate Catherine Pugh pledged to restore the city's integrity. Baltimore struggled with corruption, entrenched economic inequality, and pervasive violence for decades. Pugh pitched her slogan (moving Baltimore forward) to a city desirous of change. Indeed, the city needed a mayor dedicated to integrity and professionalism.

Previous experiences with recent Baltimore leaders were met with fraud and corruption. Pugh, on the other hand, appeared to understand the importance of effective leadership. Soon thereafter, she denounced political ties with former Mayor Sheila Dixon who resigned from office after an embezzlement conviction.

When Pugh used Dixon's tragedy to boost her campaign, many people believed she recognized the importance of resolving Baltimore's urgent problems. Others felt Pugh endured a total loss of dignity and self-respect, which made her appear shamefully weak and ineffective as a mayoral candidate. I digress:

Sheila Dixon, a beloved Mayor, was blamed for stealing gift cards meant for a city housing program. Ms.

Dixon believed the cards were personal gifts from her then-boyfriend, developer Ronald H. Lipscomb. Rumor has it, he set up Ms. Dixon as a favor. Afterward, it was discovered he had important government contracts that could not be ignored. In either case, local residents needed change.

The residents of Baltimore had been long awaiting change. Ineffective leadership in the city had been problematic since the Post-Civil Rights era began. Along the way, there were many broken promises, distrust, and neglect. Amid years of big government cover-ups and political scandals, leadership became incompetent, simply failing to produce quality services to the people.

The last Civil Rights movement shook America to the core. Black Americans were fighting against racial inequality amid reprehensible abuse committed by law enforcement. The Civil War (1865) officially abolished slavery. But it failed to end discrimination against Blacks. Blacks began to endure the devastating effects of racism (1866-1877). The devastation was especially true in the South.

By the 1940's, Black Americans experienced more than their fair share of prejudice and violence. They, along with a coalition of Whites, came together and began an unprecedented campaign to end racial inequality. The Civil Rights movement would last for two decades.

The assassination of Dr. Martin Luther King, Jr, DD caused public outrage. The Baltimore riots of 1968 would be a response that left a city war-torn. Decades later and Baltimoreans continued to be punished by the US

Government for rioting over the assassination of Dr. King. If that wasn't enough, state-sponsored violence, domestic terrorism, and government neglect worsened the situation between Whites and Blacks.

After the Baltimore riots of 2015, the government had no need to rebuild a rebellious city. However, many politicians continuously worked toward the betterment of Baltimore. There were many broken promises along the way. But no broken promise was as damning as that of former Baltimore City Mayor Catherine Pugh.

Ms. Pugh was supposed to be that beacon of hope, a new inspiration to the people. She moved to Baltimore in the 1970's to attend Morgan State University. There, she assumed a variety of roles to include work as a banker, journalist, and co-owner of two Chic Boutiques in Washington Village (Pigtown) located in southern Baltimore. Pugh would come into prominence only after serving on the City Council from 1999-2004 and the House of Delegates from 2005-2007, where she was elected to the state Senate.

Ms. Pugh would run for mayor in 2011 only to lose to Stephanie Rawlings-Blake. After learning Mayor Rawlings-Blake would not seek reelection in 2015, Pugh joined a crowd of 29 candidates in the fight to lead the City of Baltimore. Among the mayoral candidates was a wealthy businessman, a prominent Black Lives Matter activist, and a disgraced mayor who was looking for redemption.

Primary elections took place in the wake of Freddie Gray's death. The race was heated but would soon prove to be between two candidates: Pugh and Dixon. High crime and unemployment were among the many campaign issues debated as policies in need of address. Ms. Dixon pitched a campaign on her previous record of reducing crime. Her campaign slogan was based on reclaiming, reviving, and rebuilding the City of Baltimore. Pugh's message had a simple yet well-defined slogan that resonated clearly in the hearts and minds of long awaiting Baltimoreans. "Moving Baltimore forward" seemed to contradict the very presence of Sheila Dixon. It was a strong reminder of what the city tried to overcome so many times before, but failed.

Then state-appointed Senator Catherine Pugh won the primary elections. But that November, she would have to endure a spirited write-in challenge from former Mayor and disgraced politician Sheila Dixon. Unfortunately, her primary victory came with complaints about voting irregularities, including allegations of voter buyout. Perhaps Baltimore should have taken notice. But, the city was so desirous of change no one could have imagined when Pugh denied allegations, it would be among the first of many to come.

The move to city mayor permitted Pugh to benefit from Baltimore's economy. And, she had her own agenda. Pugh had the intelligence, skills, and ingenuity to follow her selfish ambitions. She would prosper in ways the city was totally unprepared for. Like any other mayor assuming responsibility for the first time, her first order of business was to take back control of the city's streets, fund public schools, housing operations, deal with corrupt local law enforcement, et cetera.

Unfortunately, there were many broken promises made during her appointment as city mayor. For example, Pugh never made good on her promise to clean up the public school system even though the City of Baltimore received financial funding from Governor Larry Hogan. She backpedalled on a few of her promises made to the city. She backpedalled so much that Governor Hogan discontinued state funding for her office. Apparently, Ms. Pugh manipulated funds to benefit herself and a select few. For Pugh, financial funding would come in the form of her Healthy Holly children's books.

The Healthy Holly Book
Series Scandal

Four Healthy Holly children's books were published by former Baltimore City Mayor Catherine Elizabeth Pugh in 2011 to 2017, including Healthy Holly: Exercising is Fun and Healthy Holly: Fruits Come in Colors Like the Rainbow. She used the money to fund her mayoral campaign. Yet, her books were never sold in stores or through wholesalers. Her book series became the center of a political scandal. The scandal prompted her resignation in May of 2019. As a result, Ms. Pugh was indicted on federal charges amid her self-published books. Ms. Pugh defrauded buyers of her Healthy Holly children's books.

On November 21, 2019, Ms. Pugh pleaded guilty to four of the 11 charges, including conspiracy to commit wire fraud, conspiracy to defraud the US government, and two counts of tax evasion. US Attorney Robert Hur said,

"Pugh's guilty plea showed she betrayed the trust placed in her by the public." Pugh faced thirty-five years in prison when sentenced February 27, 2020. She endured a total loss of dignity and self-respect.

Baltimore has had a problem with ineffective leadership for decades. The problem was city residents suffered from a gross deterioration of personal, familial, and communal relations. The nature of these relations, often fragile and difficult to sustain, laid the groundwork for unhealthy development of group cohesion and solidarity among them. It also caused a lack of moral and courageous commitment to any causes considered greater than family or one's self.

At that point in time, Baltimore communities were lost. Many families were in distress. City residents were at odds not only among themselves but with local authorities. This situation played a large role in the dishonest exploitation of power displayed by the city over the course of decades. In this way, discrimination would have no true face to include or exclude anyone on the basis of race. For decades past, it would appear Baltimore City residents were victims of their own fiendish deeds. Yet, these fiendish deeds were the results of a lack of communal resources, resources needed to help residents cope in the face of overwhelming adversity. However, what appeared to be a lack of communal resources might just have been bureaucratic corruption taking place at the level of local government.

Effective leadership does not come from the best quality genes though having good genes do help. It is not the results of accidental good fortunes. Nor is it a series of unfortunate events that guide some unsuspecting person to direct a following at the right moment in time, either. Rather, it is the result of *heritage*, traditions passed down throughout generations, that shape and mold individuals into principled people who guide or direct others in a charismatic way.

But, there can be no cohesion or solidarity without some resistance or nonconformity to policies that avoid change. There can only be polite posturing or courteous behaviors extended in kindness. Without a vibrant community to help build and shape one's values, there can be no moral commitment to any people regardless of common background, only loyalty to self. Without moral commitment, there can be no concern for strangers and others. People would refuse to create the types of relationships that forge bonds with new generations who were willing to work toward a cause or movement to ensure community wellness. In this way, only conservative efforts can be made.

In thinking about cases of bureaucratic corruption in Baltimore, Maryland, cases involving former Mayor Catherine Pugh, former Mayor Sheila Dixon, and even beloved Mayor William Donald Schaeffer whose only crime was developing conservative values, we begin to understand why it is so important for us to develop good sustainable community ties in America. The need for individuality stunts our commitment to moral development and community wellness. The absence or lack of commitment comes from a loss of personal commitment to struggles that encourage goodness and decency when others choose to conform. For now, talk of building effective leadership from what could only be called lost communities, broken down neighborhoods, and abandoned city blocks sounds a bit like empty rhetoric.

What makes a politician corrupt? What corrupts a politician? Some people say its dishonesty. Others say it's dishonesty for personal gain. Still, more say its dishonest exploitation of power usually for personal gain. In some way or another, each person is correct. But how far does corruption go? Does corruption become increasingly complex and problematic as it develops or unfolds?

How Far Does Corruption Go?

A Harford County Delegate, Mary Ann Lisanti, called Prince George's County an expletive district. She used the N-word to characterize the historically Black county in conversation with colleagues. The conversation took place in January of 2019 at a cigar bar in Annapolis, Maryland. Several legislators who were there told Darryl Barnes, chairman of the Legislative Black Caucus of Maryland, that Ms. Lisanti used a racial epithet. Caucus members called for her resignation.

Mr. Barnes felt that Ms. Lisanti's language was dated and offensive. He believed that under the circumstances she could no longer remain in office. Mr. Barnes praised the Maryland House of Delegates for their unanimous vote to censure Ms. Lisanti. Their censure vote strengthened official requests for her resignation from the Legislative Black Caucus of Maryland and the Maryland Legislative Latino Caucus, important political offices she held as a State Delegate.

The Democratic speaker of the state's House of Delegates, Michael E. Busch, stripped Ms. Lisanti of her position as chairwoman of the Unemployment Insurance Subcommittee. Given the complexity of the situation, he also removed her from the House of Economic Matters Committee after the censure vote. Ms. Liasanti finally apologized after announcing she would step down from her leadership position to participate in sensitivity training.

There was no doubt in the minds of anyone that Ms. Liasanti would misuse her authority to disadvantage Blacks and other minorities given the offensive nature of her language. In fact, given the current state of affairs, removing Ms. Liasanti from office was the appropriate choice to make.

We've witnessed a rise in hate-crime activity since Donald Trump began to hire his administration. Each member of his administration had a personal and professional history of displaying hostility toward minorities. And now that there is the potential of domestic threat arising across America, politicians have to cross every "T" and dot every "I" to ensure the safety of each and every citizen in America.

How did we come to this point in time, when we're confronted with high volumes of corruption? In one way or another, Americans have always dealt with corruption, at every level of US Government even. Slavers, members of slave patrols, even abolitionists in the Pre-Civil War period; opportunists, military generals, and bureaucrats during the Reconstruction period; bankers and business developers, even judges, sheriffs, and bounty-hunters in the era of Jim Crow segregation, especially in the early settlement of western United States. Law enforcement, politicians, and other bureaucratic officials from World War I to the new millennium and beyond, each serve as examples of how corruption can become a part of an elite system.

The Dishonesty And Fraudulent Look Of Today's Leaders

Corruption reveals the dishonesty and fraudulent look of today's leaders. Edward T. Norris would join a long list of bureaucratic and government officials who were convicted of corruption. His in your face, blunt style of talking appealed to then-Baltimore's Mayor Martin Joseph O'Malley. Norris' ability to command people made him a prime candidate for police commissioner.

He appeared to be respectful, open-minded, and had no need to draw excessive attention to himself or his status. And more pointedly, Norris appeared to be the type of man who cared. In stark contrast, the absence of humility displayed on the job by Norris was more-so characterized as an exaggerated sense of self-importance and superiority to other people. In this context, Norris was confined to police matters mainly relating to his career.

A third-generation New York cop, Norris came to Baltimore to be the city's police commissioner. He was a twenty year veteran of the New York Police Department. He would later be appointed to the Maryland State Police as Superintendent only to be convicted of corruption. He was charged with misappropriating funds from the department's expense account. He used the funds for illicit purposes, particularly drugs, prostitution, and racketeering. He entered a plea of guilty and was sentenced to six months in federal prison.

The shabby business suit worn by former Baltimore City Police Commissioner Darryl De Sousa at the start of his trial not only represented the age that shaped and molded him, it also disclosed the duplicity of high profiled corruption and the practice of deliberately making people believe his innocence. De Sousa was also charged with corruption. He was sentenced to ten months in federal prison for failing to file three years of federal tax returns.

The standard, near marginal style of clothing worn by most leaders today can be said to show how unimportant they feel about their service to the public and the level of incompetence that exist in serving the US Government. For De Sousa, that humbling image of a top cop lifestyle was critical if he was to convince a jury that his selfish ambitions were the direct results of him being undermined as a public servant. Curiously, yesterday's leaders had a higher aptitude for truth and justice, followed a code of conduct, and were guided by moral action.

But, how does that make us accountable for the behaviors of people like Edward T. Norris, Darryl De Sousa, and Catherine Pugh? How do we come to terms with low caliber political performances of people like Stephanie Rawlings-Blake who assumed office on the coattail of her father, Howard Peters "Pete" Rawlings? As I try to point out "in press," Blacks account for an increasingly large amount of corruption since the Post-Civil Rights era. And with the amount of scandals increasing in government, we're likely to see more well within the next two decades.

But how does today's corruption differentiate from the corruption of yesterday? The US Government is so corrupt today, it's more like business as usually for politicians and elected officials whereas yesterday's leaders felt there was something to lose from violating one's oath of office. Needless to say, many people believe this reasoning holds true. Still, much of what is good about the US Government—that is to say, any laws, policies, or personal attributes that enable politicians to lead effectively—is more noticeable in Blacks and other minorities.

We saw examples of goodness in Former President Barrack Obama who led the country with compassion. We saw the power of effective leadership in Congressman John Lewis who, after tireless lobbying efforts, built the African American Museum located in Washington, DC. And let us not forget "the Squad," four minority Congresswomen who stormed Congress with their grassroots approach to politics in 2018. These great feats were performed by minority politicians who believed in social change.

We see in many of our minority leaders a sense of mission. They are inspired in their sacrifice and commitment to admire, serve, and lead everyday, ordinary people. These public servants have a deep sense of community. They understand they're connected to people who share a common history, a history that is part of their heritage, their tradition. And they understand traditions are the building blocks that lead to the successful roles of minorities in today's society.

Mainstream leaders, who follow the status quo, are too full of compromise to give good people hope, confidence, or courage about life matters. Like any other politician, they are concerned about winning the next election, maintaining their following, and recruiting people to finance their campaign. What they fail to understand is you cannot celebrate a party victory without motivating people to vote. And, without the momentum necessary to develop an ever-growing constituency, there can be no cause or forward push for equality.

What We Can Do About It

What we can do about it is resolve the perpetually thorny problem of bureaucratic corruption. It is as easy as removing ineffective leadership. But first, in order to rid the country of its ineffective leaders, we must openly admit to ourselves a *"denial of weakness."* This problem, denial of weakness, is the Achilles' heel of our time. It may seem our weaknesses are small. But, it makes us fatally vulnerable, much like a neurological glitch in one's thinking or a chink in one's body armor. *Denial of weakness* is a mindset marked by a refusal or an inability to underscore the importance of dealing with serious political issues.

To understand denial of weakness is to improve our understanding of limitations. Each generation needs to improve on accepting our limitations to create more competent leaders. That way, those who are ineffectual can readily be identified. That is to say, we must begin to or make an effort to understand, accept, and deal with the idea that our nation's leaders lack the ability to perform their duties.

Incompetence is a problem of ability or one of moral character. It is defined by the intricacies of child rearing or good upbringing. There's always a chance to better generations through good upbringing. It ensures that each generation is more competent than the previous. In that way, each generation gets a better chance to improve not only themselves, but their surrounding environment.

In a competent society—just like a mechanic who replaces bad parts with new parts until the machine is in finely tuned working order—societal members can replace ineffective leaders with new, more competent leaders until the system works well for everyone. In this way, it's not a far stretch to remove ineffective leaders from leadership roles and start anew. Unlike the Trump administration where his members are in deep denial about his weaknesses, it has to begin by recognizing or acknowledging there is a real problem in political leadership.

Then, we need to identify the problem by its distinctive characteristic features. That means we have to ask what makes a leader weak and thus ineffectual. It could be a fault in the way they safeguard themselves that makes leaders vulnerable to exploitation. For example, it could be an aspect of their character or a point in their argument. Corruption is well defined by one's moral character and readily witnessed in the argument one makes.

We should also look at appearance since it creates lasting impressions. Impressions have everything to do with charisma. We know leaders are charismatic, often affecting people in their thinking or actions by means of argument, example, or force of personality. Democrats are in utter surprise by the impression Donald Trump left on the course of twenty-first century American culture. Rather, they are impressed with his lasting effects on generating a sense of community among a forgotten people. The best example of this ability to impress others is in his campaign slogan, Make America Great Again (MAGA).

His slogan is twofold in bringing awareness to people America had long since forgotten and in creating unity or solidarity among them. These modes of awareness and solidarity lay the ground work for group cohesion and are guided by the appearance of compassion. For my purposes, his slogan can be construed as a phrase that brought harmony of opinion, interest, or feeling together in a display of tender affection to a people otherwise forgotten by society.

His message brings feelings of hope to those who are looking for critical affirmation of dignity. We find self-affirming dignity not just in White identity extremists, but your everyday, ordinary, working class White citizen who struggles for acknowledgement in a society where the individual feels like he or she has little to no control over their lives let alone the menace behind bureaucratic corruption.

Weaknesses take place at every level of US Government. But, we should focus on local government where civil society continues to be in thrall to big government. Weaknesses arise at state and federal levels. It occurs when big government is confronted by grassroots democratic organizations. These organizations build cohesive programs with leadership who gain respect from opposing organizations. This cohesion epitomizes all that is right, fair, or just with it and other democratically housed grassroots organizations.

Like the members of Post-Party conservatism, critics who deny weakness never acknowledge that it ultimately shapes their aversion to change. Yet, unlike conservatism, advocates would not allow their weaknesses to avoid corruption, but to confront bureaucratic corruption. Much like Libertarianism, critics argue against weaknesses in their organizations while they claim people should have complete freedom of thought and action.

Unlike Libertarianism, advocates argue liberals believe in the doctrine of free will but refuse to argue equal rights for Black people due to weaknesses in their belief system. *Denial of weakness* is our way of refusing to recognize and deal with serious policy issues—policy issues that could ultimately reshape our cultural identity. It is a way of being concerned with our own interests, needs, and wishes while ignoring those of others.

In addition, denial of weakness prevents us from shining a light on bureaucratic corruption. The problem is it does not allow us to stay in touch with everyday, ordinary people in the community. It also prevents us from connecting to ordinary members of an organization who live in modest communities, communities where ordinary people and community leaders continue to call out bureaucratic corruption in their fight for equality.

Chapter 4
A Sign of the Times

The white man's happiness cannot be purchased by the black man's misery

Frederick Douglass (1818 – 1895)

We live in one of the most troubling and frustrating times ever. The murder rate is at an all time high. Black children are abducted at an average of twenty-eight hundred a year. Organ harvesting is a global problem, especially across the African Diaspora. Political corruption is ramped. Segregated, low income neighborhoods have the highest crime rates in America. These crimes—because the citizens living in poor neighborhoods are low priority—are made to look normal. The result is Blacks are afraid they will soon become a permanent underclass. Though I'm not sure, it may be a sign of the times.

The problem is we've lost the idea of community. We follow the belief that society exists for the rights and benefits of individuals. Slavery, racism, and segregation contributed to America's unhealthy preoccupation with self-serving values. Minorities are disproportionately affected in this way. People unknowingly make decisions that serve themselves in ways other people might view as selfish or indefensible. They're often taught that personal needs and wishes are more important than those of others. The resultant attitude is the pursuit of personal happiness and independence rather than collective goals or interests.

I'm not talking about being constrained by government interventions or made subordinate to collective interests. I am talking about making personal investments in one's community. Your time, energy, or effort to undertaking a community activity or project is essential to achieving true sovereignty or independence. At a crucial time when Blacks are on the verge of becoming a permanent underclass, they appear to no longer be interested in sacrificing themselves to better their community.

It's a lot to ask of people, I know. But, the idea of self-serving values blinds us in ways whereby we put our personal needs and desires ahead of others. Now, I'm not asking for people to live under impossibly ideal conditions where everyone lives in harmony and everything is for the best. But, in order to achieve community wellness, people must have access to a combination of social, economical, environmental, cultural, and political systems identified as essential for them to flourish and fulfill their potential.

Many of our nation's leaders are taught to put personal concerns and interests ahead of others. They have a tendency to seek out personal goals and use it in ways that advance their own needs and desires. Why? Self-serving values show that personal needs and desires make people feel enthusiastic, interested, and committed to succeed.

The problem is self-serving values block ambitions thereby causing even the most well-intentioned persons to completely overlook their own indiscretions. Unfortunately, not all self-interest can be gratified. Hence, there is a ten year expiration date ending the fixed period for which honesty comes to an end and politicians can no longer be trusted. Thus, we have the emergent of people like Mike

Bloomberg who apologized for his inappropriate past actions in ways that was tactless and unwise.

State of the Nation

The MAGA supporters won the 2016 US Presidential Elections. And, Democrats continued to be bothered by the Electoral College's decision, provoked by conservatives and their discomfort, uneasiness, and fear of change. We're now feeling the effects of right-winged extremism that began largely after President-elect Donald Trump was sworn into the Oval Office as America's forty-fifth US President.

We're also confronted with a redistribution of wealth from working class citizens to the cultural elite. In 2013, President Obama increased taxes for the wealthiest Americans. Many felt a tax hike would affect their livelihood. It did not! Today, many are fearful another tax increase would slow down their income growth or hurt the economy. Thus, they are in a panic over fear of having another tax increase.

Late entry Billionaire Mike Bloomberg was admitted into the 2020 US presidential race as a Democratic candidate, and thanks to his status, power, and wealth. Unfortunately, oligarchs are who you get when conservatives from the cultural elite are exposed to any hint of change. It is a pandemic moment when they reveal themselves in their warped attempts to renew hope. And with plutocrats likes Donald Trump leading the country, more of the superrich are beginning to run for US President.

We're in the fight of our lives as people are pulled in different directions by various voices and visions on the claim of change. For so long, we looked at Republicans as right, true, and just, and to overcome our circumstances. But, they pulled us into a destabilized political situation. Yet, there is renewed hope in the voices and continued visions of progressivism.

Progressives ask how do we gain or retain certain sources of hope and vision while vulnerable to conservatism? Conservatism is what happens when political institutions or systems become faulty, ineffective, or unjust. It is in that moment—when a country is under siege by political factions having interests or beliefs that are not always aligned with the larger party—that we must ask ourselves how do we view our present situation and often while bashed by right-winged propaganda and provoked by media's negative appeal to change? The answer is simple enough: align yourself with supporters or advocates of social, economical, or political reforms. They'll be the ones who are willing to reorganize and improve the current situation, especially in social or political spheres. In any event, America turned to progressivism for renewed hope or change.

Bernie Sanders is a blast from the past. Perhaps, the most progressive, this US Democratic frontrunner, renewed hope by inspiring generations to advocate for an end to privatized healthcare and the exploitation of working class citizens, many among the working poor. At a time when capitalism feels more like communism, as I do believe, Bernie has promised a political revolution, saying both parties are obliged, grateful, and indebted to corporate money.

Corporate greed is a political ill. However, corporations perform many functions of private businesses, governments, educational bodies, and various professions. The problem is corporate executives often line their pockets with money levied by government on its citizens. Corporations also ensure lawmakers prepare legislation to favor its members. For example, Trump's tax cuts helped the superrich pay fewer taxes than working class citizens in 2018 and that's a big problem. Typically, the superrich pay lower taxes than the working class. And that needs to stop!

Bernie Sanders wants to make corporations pay their fair share. For too long, greedy corporate executives have fixed the tax code, killed market competition, and outright oppressed people and communities across America. Every year, we've watched paid wages reduced, countless workers laid off, and businesses closed down, all while corporate elites indulge themselves in huge bonuses. Typically, they escape legal prosecution by appealing to a broken campaign finance system where a few large campaign donations can buyout any politician. But, when the stock market crashed in 2008, President George W. Bush signed the Emergency Economic Stabilization Act. The seven hundred billion dollar bank bailout is a classic example of the corruption and fraudulent behavior conducted by corporate elites, typically in the use of quid pro quo.

In a similar turn of events, former Mayor and disgraced politician Catherine E. Pugh received her sentencing on March 27, 2020. In receiving a three year sentence for fraud, tax evasion, and conspiracy, many people felt Ms. Pugh deserved the stiffest penalty. And with new charges handed out to her after the fact, she personified the dysfunction of government long believed by Baltimore City residents, which strengthened distrust in their hearts and minds.

When we talk about crime or criminal behavior, we think about people who act contrary to the law. But, when we're haunted by political corruption, there is a wicked dishonesty that allows for the exploitation of power and the thought of it becomes too much to bear. That someone could be unscrupulous enough to put an entire community in harm's way, and for personal gain, is mortifying. Like in the case of the Electoral College voting into office a corrupt capitalist like Donald Trump, there is a genuine feeling of helplessness and hopelessness that consumes the public. And I'm not talking just about Trump. People are more often devastated whenever there is corruption in politics.

Among minorities, there is talk about voting for the lesser of two evils. Whenever a Republican holds a political office, there is a deep feeling of grief and despair that consumes minorities. Remember, Bernie said both parties were unrestrained by moral or ethical principles. Bernie is a sign of the times, an aspiration of new hope. Perhaps, he is a sign that times are changing. What I hope and pray for is he never gets reduced to the point of political corruption. Politics has it way of changing people from better to worst. Given ten years and even the most well-intentioned person will become corrupt under the activities associated with politics, especially someone who assumes political activities as a profession.

When the people of Maryland voted former Mayor William Donald Schaefer into office as Governor, they had the audacity to hope change would come. Schaefer was a beloved Mayor who looked after the citizens of Baltimore. He served Baltimore for most of the time he was in public office. If someone like him could be corrupt by upper echelons in Annapolis, Maryland, it is more than enough to turn people away from hope, truly a sign of the times.

Politicians may make speeches that appeal to the masses. But, these speeches are more often codified to entice supporters or advocates of conservatism. Minorities may feel comfortable with politicians making persuasive speeches about the current state of affairs. But, how well-off are they really? Too many people seem to be well-adjusted to injustice. For too long, there has been no one willing to fight back against the tyranny of oppression. Not since Civil Rights greats like Dr. Martin Luther King, Jr., Malcolm X, and Ida B. Wells-Barnett, had we champions to take up the cause for poor and vulnerable people who fought against the multilevel assault on our poorest and most vulnerable.

The Time Is Right!

The time is right for a union of interest, purpose, or sympathy. There must be a collective effort to achieve change, especially by way of political or social reform. It does not have to be a revelation or Democratic awakening that focuses on poor and vulnerable people, either. I'm not sure about older generations, whether they have the courage to stand up and fight. But, these younger generations are more than willing and able.

These younger generations are visibly upset about their situation. They are at the limits of their patience, the point at which they have run out of options or are so frustrated that they can no longer cope with oppression. They are more than willing to make a collective effort to effect change in social thinking. They spent quite a few years being groomed for that moment in time when they would stand up and fight back against oppression.

For more than two decades, Generation X prepared to stand up and fight back against the multilevel assault on our nation's poor and most vulnerable. It was a time of great consciousness for them. In fact, they took back city streets, wiped out East Coast gang violence, and through its reemerge, instilled a new found sense of consciousness in each other. And, talk about when ordinary people wake up, their movement was so conscious, it had to be outlawed by the powers that be.

Though their efforts were interrupted, nearly stifled, the movement transcended across racial boundaries and across world cultures. It survives in White America, throughout the Northern hemisphere, even in Great Britain where the Queen has broken away from the European Union, and various parts of Asia. Although remnants of it continues in the Black community, it started generations of protesters, anarchists, resisters, and nonconformists, many of whom fight on the front lines of Democracy at present.

It takes courage to stand up and fight. True! But to stand for a cause greater than yourself takes audacity. Let it be known the younger generation will not be deterred from their course of action. Many people from older generations were taught proper etiquettes. Those rules responsible for governing correct or polite behavior in society or in specific social or professional settings allowed them to mask their true selves. The younger generation was never taught to develop such a persona only "the importance of being yourself" as it was instilled into the moral character of my generation (Generation X).

Your persona is often designed to help you achieve in your chosen course of action. In the process, people often get lost and confused about their true identity. And while they may not be overcome by fear, their persona more often allows them to retreat from a previous stand on any matter, which means they avoid inevitability.

The younger generation, needing no mask to wear, is more candid about their feelings. Thus, they are defensible. You might call it being soft or overly emotional. Why, because they will not endure. In fact, older generations are indefensible, a problem of wearing too many mask. While older generations endure or engage in complacent slumber—all the while asking themselves why dominant society always get away with this level of abuse; why do they subjugate our people; why do they exploit us—youngsters from Generation Y said we cannot allow them to get away with domination. And, in one fell swoop, they gained enough momentum to become a power-base.

Generation Y was never taught to mask their identity for a role better suited or appropriate for the outside world. In the age of tattoos, body piercings, and natural hairstyles, the right to live life without being subject to insult, harm, or domination by existing powers is worth courage, commitment, and sacrifice. For them, the danger, difficulty, uncertainty, or pain of being oppressed is real. Anything else is unrealistic. So, for them to stand up and fight is quite natural.

The problem was their planning method lacked organization. In fact, they failed to effectively mobilize their resources. An example of this was witnessed in the Baltimore Riots of 2015. Outraged citizens expressed strong opposition to state-sponsored violence and antiblack racism. They caused public disturbances during which a mob of angry grade school students took to the streets in open protest. Their actions spurred more protest and violence. Rioting resulted in looting, arson, and vandalism. What they needed was to come together to form an agenda.

What Black Americans learned from rioting was how to make better use of available people in order to form public demonstrations and other such actions.

Such methods involved nonviolent disobedience, political mobilization of resources, and moral suasion to mobilize public opinion.

It would take some doing to get a true movement started. But, with the killing sprees sanctioned by the state, the movement was bound to happen. At present, sixty activist groups joined Black Lives Matter to set their agenda during a round of negotiations with government officials.

You see, there's never been a question of courage for the younger generation. Their problem has always been one of focus or direction. These young adults never had conscious control over their lifestyle. Without true discipline to mask lesser parts of their character and personality, they lacked the ability to impose efficient working methods to start important movements. It would take some time for them to organize into the types of activist groups we see and appreciate today. But, nevertheless, it's the younger generation who is on the front lines of the Black Lives Matter movement, so called because most of the movements of today center around saving Black lives.

When Dr. King was assassinated, it put an end to the Civil Rights movement. And with that, his death killed the characteristic spirit of culture. Dominant society feared the movement was becoming fashionable or popular and attracting increasing support as a blame culture. His assassination would bring the Black liberation struggle to an abrupt end. So, the government created a process that would help them to prevent another serious Black push against a White power-base. At the same time, the Government would commend King's courage, struggle, and sacrifice as a commemoration of his commitment to the movement.

Many governments, world cultures, and societies felt America did not have the capacity to treat Black people with dignity and decency. The US Government could no longer afford to sit back and do nothing. The fear was racial inequality would in some way affect relations with world cultures. Rumor has it, the world wanted to conduct business with Black people, not White Americans. So, the Civil Rights movement had to end. The world was watching. People abroad were becoming sympathetic. Leading cultures would not stand for social, ethnic, racial, or economic disparities to continue between cultural systems.

People say they understand where the younger generation is coming from. If only they could find a better approach to addressing race matters, they would agree to participate in their movement. Many people believe the problem with today's generation is they're too wild or unruly. However, every generation has its quirks. The point is their demeanor is apparently what's needed to fight back against oppression. In fact, their all in for doing whatever it takes to get the job done. And that is to be applauded.

What We Can Do About It

Bernie Sanders has strong convictions about the state of this nation. Could a government benefit from promoting the actions of its citizens at the expense or consideration of others? The United States is one country clearly trying to promote White supremacy. Unfortunately, Americans have mixed opinions on the matter. Without question, there is class bias as well as racial bias in American leadership by whom the poor and most vulnerable are greatly disadvantaged.

Both dominant society and lobbying groups have made it difficult for race-related legislation to be approved. President Barack Obama signed legislation for the Matthew Shepard and James Byrd, Jr. Hate Crimes Act, which passed into law on October 28, 2009. But it was a modest law, greatly in need of revision. The degree of respect for a government and the appropriateness of its actions are important factors in whether people will abide by legal constraints to promote community wellness.

That being said, lawmakers who introduce or maintain these legislations should be highly respected members in the community. For example, Congressman Elijah Cummings was a highly successful and respected politician in the City of Baltimore. He encouraged residents to be vigilant about corruption and police abuse but also reminded people that communities and law enforcement work best when united. Operation Crime Watch was designed to prevent and reduce criminal activity in Baltimore City by creating and supporting neighborhood-based block watch and citizen patrol programs through a partnership between city residents, the Mayor's Office on Criminal Justice, the Baltimore City Police Department, and the Washington/Baltimore High Intensity Drug Trafficking Area (HIDTA).

Any residents of Baltimore can support or gain the support of police officers in the prevention and reduction of crime through open means of communication and by developing problem-solving techniques adapted for improving community relations. Residents have not taken advantage of this program largely because the Baltimore City Police Department (BPD) is not highly respected in Baltimore's Black communities. They have a long history of abusing young Black males dating back generations. Some are member of hate groups; and, many more are not from the greater Baltimore area.

So far, in this chapter and others, we have seen that dominant society clearly has greater status, power, and wealth. Such disparities are what led to the stratification of our social, economical, and political systems. Our social stratification system provides complexity for the way in which poor and vulnerable people are perceived, especially how Black people are treated. In addition, "the system" is involved in the actual development of health and wellness in the Black community. Together with health and wellness, status, power, and wealth relate to one another.

Chapter 5
Black Lives Matter

For more than 500 years Black people have been fighting for our freedom. We have fought back against slavery, Black codes, Jim Crow laws, policing, incarceration, some of the highest unemployment rates, consistent homelessness, dying while giving birth, being murdered for being trans or non-binary. We have been the consistent moral compass in a country that has thrived on harming the most vulnerable of its population.

Patrisse Khan-Cullors (2019)

In 2012, I would begin to write about one of America's most unspoken truths. As the focus of public discourse, my purpose was to raise awareness about problems affecting Black people. Since then, the Black community witnessed very senseless and tragic deaths. Trayvon Martin, Michael Brown, Eric Garner, Sandra Bland, and a great many Black people from the younger generation died needlessly and senselessly due to state-sanctioned violence and antiblack racism. This chapter will look at a call to action that led to one of the biggest modern freedom movements in American history.

The Black Lives Matter movement (#BLM) was born in the face of criticism. It started in response to an acquittal of George Zimmerman, the man who shot and killed 17-year-old Trayvon Martin. The movement was created as an ideological and political intervention to prevent the further demise of Black Americans. Alicia Garza, Patrisse Cullors, and Opal Tometi, its founders, said the Black Lives Matter movement was an affirmation of Black humanity, their contributions to this great nation, and a testament of Black people's remarkable resilience and adaptation shown over the centuries.

I wrote about Trayvon Martin's murder in The Ignoble Paradox of Man. And I must say, for me, the most disturbing aspect of his murder was neither the trial nor the fact a jury would acquit a grown man of murdering a child. Instead, it was the callous comments dominant society made, including terrorist threats directed at Black Americans, and in support of Zimmerman simply because he was a White Hispanic biracial. Other victims of antiblack violence include but are not limited to Tamir Rice, Tanisha Anderson, Mya Hall, and Walter Scott. Inherently important names for the movement because it encouraged serious discussions about the state-sanctioned violence they endured.

I also examined the misery and wretchedness of suffering found to exist among Blacks and their families in addition to the entire premise surrounding state-sanctioned violence. This near frightening discovery comes from White discomfort, uneasiness, and fear of change. It is the increasing motivation behind the hash-tag Black Lives Matter.

Somehow, in some way, dominant society fears constant change will lead America to function in fundamentally different ways. Well-established families with resources and community ties were quick to perceive sociocultural differences as a problem source. They condemn any activities that may alter their lifestyles even though they know nothing about the people or their social backgrounds. They are disappointed about changes that appear beyond their control.

The notion of a changing demographic tapestry seems to justify the brutal mistreatment of Black people. Widespread violence of Blacks in America is a sad fact. The oppressive effects of our current state of affairs leads to racial divisions with dominant society content to focus on preserving the status quo and distracted against working toward social change. They appear to be listless and inactive in their quest to move forward toward liberal racial attitudes. Instead, they appear to be greatly resistant toward instigating any changes that may result in loss of identity or status. Their unbending, pitiless resistance removes from possibility any real hope of bettering this great nation.

Black people have no reason to be hopeful given the current state of affairs. Racial inequality and social injustice has indeed plagued this great nation of ours. Dominant society sacrificed their principles for the sake of power and control. Their fear was, and still is, losing White privilege, losing grounds as a majority, or that the economic gap is closing between White, Black, and Latino people. Due to dominant society and their discomfort, uneasiness, and fear, it was always the intent of Black Lives Matter's foundational members to bring together Black communities across the African Diaspora, any Black community that shared a desire for justice.

The goal of Black Lives Matter was twofold. First, it was the intention of their program to give active help and encouragement to young and upcoming Black leaders. Secondly, they wanted to create a network that would give

Black people a greater sense of confidence or the drive to determine their own ambitions. The motivation for their goals was, and will always be, the widespread and deliberate violence inflicted on Black people, violence sanctioned by the US government.

Black Lives Matter (#BLM) has a deep moral commitment to placing marginal groups closer to the center of liberation. In addition to organizing projects and motivating others, #BLM recognized and acknowledged significant problems in past movements. These problems were compounded by the types of people who actually led these movements and the near bigoted disposition of their leadership.

Past liberation movements all but failed to reach everyday, ordinary people. These movements often neglected to include women, lesbians, gays, and other minorities as part of their cause. As a network, it has always been the intention of #BLM to include members from all walks of life into the liberation movement.

Black Lives Matter has always supported and endorsed women and members of LGBTQ. Many have taken on leadership roles in the movement toward liberation. Not once has Black Lives Matter created exclusionary policies that would prevent anyone from participating in the liberation of a culture, group, or its members.

A Call to Action

Back then (2013-2014), millions of Americans were influenced by the fictitious excitements of media sensationalism. People were in the habit of not only listening to but believing in the most lurid, shocking, and controversial aspects of Black life in America, especially as represented by network television. But the thrill of media sensationalism abruptly came to an end when the residents of Missouri received a reality check.

Public demonstrations were held in Ferguson, Missouri after a White police officer fatally shot an unarmed Black teenager. Residents and political activists met at a public gathering in rally against Ferguson's latest victim. Later the same day, residents began walking in a march to express strong opposition to White police abuse of authority. As protests continued, clashes and riots ensued. What the state of Missouri did not realize was the tragic event helped to catalyze an already growing popular anger existing among Black Americans.

Black Lives Matter (#BLM), a newly formed activist group, set out to Ferguson, Missouri on a Freedom Ride. Their mission was to march for justice in the name of Michael Brown, the Black teenager who was fatally shot by police officer Darren Wilson. Ferguson was a reminder of what they were supposed to be fighting for. The activist group pledged its commitment to people whose lives had been divided or disrupted by state-sanctioned violence and antiblack racism, people like Trayvon Martin. No one could have anticipated the impact Ferguson would have on the country.

Ferguson was the catalyst that accelerated the growth and potential of #BLM. The activist group would return home and make a collective effort to build the foundation for what would soon become their global network. Black Lives Matter Global Network Infrastructure would forever change the characteristic spirit of the movement. In the early beginnings of its global network project, #BLM quickly became home to many people who shared the same political agenda.

It's hard for people to understand the true significance of #BLM let alone fully comprehend what it means to be a global network. Most of us are completely controlled by the dominance of conservatism while others the sheer absurdity of what it means to be liberal in America. The fact that the Federal Bureau of Investigation (FBI) branded Black Lives Matter an identity extremist group tells us we are totally controlled by the deep xenophobic nature of political conservatism. The unfair use of statements about an identity group in order to influence the actions or attitudes of an entire nation is characteristic conservatism.

Aversion to change (conservatism) prevents us from having deep meaningful discussions on how much Black lives actually matter to the American people. The astonishing and much needed appearance of #BLM—in political protests, public events, and in political rallies— tells us how disturbing it is to truly have a decent dialogue on problems affecting Black lives in America. That for some people the very nature of Black lives was extremely troubling because most felt like Blacks were unworthy of public consideration.

Black Lives Matter understood that in order for the government to solve identity problems, minorities must first have access to America's social system. This idea doesn't mean more public assistant programs. Government mandated programs cover one dimension of the social system. It also doesn't mean changing the behavior of minorities so they can be useful for White production. Those ideas suggest minorities function contrary to accepted moral principles.

It also removes from possibility the idea of public accountability. What that means is the government refuses to be held responsible for atrocities it committed against its own people, a people who continue to be victimized. What they need is for the government to give them an opportunity or the right to experience and make use of America's social, economical, and political systems.

In fact, the real problem is liberals and conservatives, Democrats and Republicans, consider minorities (specifically Black Americans) to be burdensome rather than a people who were and continue to be exploited, oppressed, and humiliated by their own government. Black Lives Matter refused to allow Americans to view Black people as economic burdens when America is responsible for their predicament.

By advocating in support of Black people, #BLM hoped to bring awareness to a volatile situation where

Whites once denied having committed crimes against Black people. What it also does for the movement is allow them to show their leaders no one involved is entirely blameless. Similarly, it also shows that for conservatives to place the entire blame on Black folk—by not answering to their role in Black oppression—they continue to harbor malice toward them. Black Lives Matter also recognizes when leadership benefit at the expense or consideration of others. Now, I do understand no one involved in the process is entirely blameless. But understand, whenever leadership separates its members from problems where they continue to benefit, it is a denial of justice.

Black Lives Matter does not consider racial divisions to be inevitable digressions of society but constitutive elements of life. While liberals believe in integrating minorities into mainstream society, conservatives do not see the need to absorb them into their way of living. Both are wrong because either method requires minorities to accommodate the cultural mainstream. Yet, the idea of assimilating or integrating minorities into a cultural mainstream is defensible in that it's an inevitable progression of evolution. People should be fully integrated or, at least, assimilated into all mainstreams regardless of race, ethnicity, gender, religion, or social class.

A Global Network

In order for Black Lives Matter to address the problem of antiblack racism in America, they concentrated their efforts not on problems within the Black community but the differential treatment of Blacks by dominant society—inequalities that lay at the core of antiblack racism. The route they took to illicit a proper response from existing powers determined their political will. So long as Whites considered Black progression to be an "us versus them" movement, Black people would forever be saddled with the burden of providing sufficient warrant for their continued acceptance in society. The notion that only a select few have the right to pit us against them, choose who belongs and who doesn't, or decide which one of us is good versus evil, is embodied in the very Principles of Machiavelli.

That strong Black identities can emerge in the face of deadly oppression, especially young Black women, is a testament of their will, drive, and sheer determination to make a place for themselves in a begrudging society. Strong progressive views held by important figures like Coretta Scott King throughout her lifetime to those of Toni Morison (-2019), share one commonality: that all citizens of society are endowed with unalienable rights to life, liberty, and the pursuit of happiness. And until dominant society stops victimizing its minority citizens, that is to say, until there is justice for Trayvon Martin, until there is peace for Freddie Gray, until someone tells the truth about what happened in the hanging death of Sandra Bland, and until there is some accountability for the suspicious death of Detective Sean Suiter, activist groups like Black Lives Matter will continue to build and prosper.

Black Lives Matter is responsible for the largest Black liberation struggle in America. It is gallantly used as a network among activists to recover, reorganize, and prepare Black people to function independently and after having sovereignty wrested away by the oligarchy. Like the Marcus Garvey movement, it is a Black identity struggle with shared philosophies of political union across the African Diaspora. Unlike the Marcus Garvey movement, it is all inclusive, encompassing people who do not fit into a neat social category.

It's not all inclusive because it has a broad political agenda as any good liberation movement should. It's given that title due to its willingness to tolerate a wide range of ideas and behavior despite racial divisions. Black Lives Matter has the kind of forward-thinking that opens up public discussions not only on race but gender identity groups like Women, lesbians, gays, transgender, and others.

To establish a global network, #BLM had to look at the qualities or characteristics of the organization consider-ed as a whole. Next, they needed to consider the situation surrounding what it meant to be Black in America. What it meant to be Black in America was to endure chronic living conditions, systemic abuse, and mistreatment of trans and queer Blacks. Such suffering was motivation to stand up against a society that refused to acknowledge Black people's humanity. Individually, not much could be done about it. But, collectively, anything was possible. Thus, they made their stance as a united front.

The Ferguson standoff proved Black people could not only unite as a front but connect in ways that were unforeseeable. The Trayvon Martin case and the message it sent speaks volumes. They were united as a people by common interests or concerns. Today, eighty-five percent of White people are third generation descendants, meaning America is a melting pot of immigrants. Yet, enforced racial hierarchies create aversions to change. Such aversions not only prevent people from changing but, more profoundly, keep nations from evolving.

The not guilty verdict of George Zimmerman was the prelude to the Ferguson, Missouri standoff. Both cases were perceived to be wrong by the entire world. Yet, somehow, in some way, dominant society chose not to acknowledge the differential treatment or systemic abuse of Black Americans. Many of these Black folk were males from the younger generation, more of the abused were increasingly female. The callous attitude of dominant society is why Black Lives Matter Global Network began.

The damning situation of both verdicts led Black Lives Matter to play a pivotal role in uniting a people once thought could not be united. To unify people by a common interest or concern, or to become unified in this way, changed the conversation on Blackness at the dinner table. It also helped catalyze other movements throughout the nation and around the world.

The world bore witness to American violence and the threat of violence against Black people, carried out for political purposes. For those reasons, more than sixty organizations worked together with the Black Lives Matter movement to make their concerns known to those in government and to influence the passage of legislation. They released a series of policy demands. Among the lists of demands were tuition free education, reparations, and abolishing capital punishment. The policy demands were made after both Democratic and Republican National Conventions, and nearly two years after Michael Brown's death.

Montague Simmons, a representative of an activist group called the Organization for Black Struggle and the Movement for Black Lives Policy Table addressed their policy demands to the US Government. The list jutted out over police killings of Black people. It included state-sanctioned violence like the school-to-prison pipeline, declining opportunities to earn, wars waged on Black trans and queer families (as if they were not human), and a host of other inhumane acts committed against Black people.

Terror campaigns, they decreed, were the reasons Blacks stood unified. Renewed and purposeful, they wanted to put forth a shared vision not to recreate America in a fundamentally different way, but to create a reimagining of a world for their children where they could live in peace.

The plan, entitled A Vision for Black Lives: Policy Demands for Black Power, Freedom and Justice, consisted of six key demands and 40 priority policies that included putting an end to killing Black People, reparations for American Descendants of Slaves, Investment versus Divestment just to name a few. Other policy demands included but were not limited to:

> **Economic Justice**: This is calling for Black communities to have real collective ownership of wealth in the U.S. This could be achieved with restructuring tax codes, creating

federal and state job programs that specifically target the most economically marginalized Black people, breaking up large banks and ensuring better protection for workers.

Community Control: This would include the end of the privatization of education and making sure communities have the power to hire and fire officers, determine disciplinary action, control budgets and policies, and subpoena relevant agency information when needed.

Political Power: To ensure that real democracy can be achieved for all Black people, BLM wants for all political prisoners to be released, eliminating Super Pacs that fund candidates, ensuring election protection, early registration at the age of 16, full access to technology and the internet, and increased funding to HBCU's.

As the violence against Black lives continued, so did the qualities or characteristics of life considered as a whole. The lack of kindness or compassion for others eroded Black communities to a feeling of despair, despondency, or misery. The transformation of Black Lives Matter into a global network was a push to revitalize the dispiriting atmosphere of Black neighborhoods that past communities once invigorated.

In the past, Black life existed as a byproduct of Jim Crow segregation. Despite systemic inequality (displacement, exclusion, and segregation), neighboring folk came together in a push for the Commonwealth. These supportive networks helped sustain Blacks in the face of despair, disease, and death. One of the remarkable outcomes was their resilience and adaptation that led to the development of their own communities and social structures. These historically Black communities consisted of Black owned banks, Black churches, Black owned businesses, historically Black educational institutions, and many more important community resources to combat the stress and oppression of dominant society.

In addition, they learned to negotiate with dominant society. They also had a strong value system and great sense of community. Further, Blacks mastered strategies to help bring them into the mainstay of American life.

The Greenwood district of Tulsa, Oklahoma (approx. 1879 – 1921) was one of the most commercially successful and affluent communities in Black America. Called Black Wall Street, it was a self-contained hub for Black owned businesses and financial services. Other prominent Black communities that thrived in spite of segregation were the Hayti Community in Durham, North Carolina, Jackson Ward in Richmond, Virginia, The Fourth Avenue District of Birmingham, Alabama (-1950), and Boley, Oklahoma (1932), were considered divisions of Black Wall Street.

In order to help Black people sustain some sense of purpose in life, Black Lives Matter Global Network pledged to organize and rebuild independence among Blacks across the nation. They felt it was time to stimulate national interest. Hopefully, in turn, many Black people would galvanize their communities to end state-sanctioned violence and antiblack racism.

Our bastardized existence is magnificent and grows deeper and more pronounced precisely when we're put at greater risk. Given the plight and predicament of Blacks in America—state-sanctioned violence and the widespread deterioration of Black progress—has there ever been any doubt in your mind as to why so many Black people develop a cynical distrust of our bureaucratic system. Electing unqualified political candidates into high profile political positions caused this division of opinion. The Ferguson, Missouri standoff was, perhaps, the first time in post-modern history that a newly formed activist group gained enough momentum to become a power-base.

What We Can Do About It

Well, the Black Lives Matter Global Network Infrastructure continues to do its part in organizing and power building across the nation. Now that they are providing us with tools of empowerment, it is up to us to rebuild our communities and preserve integrity. Our local organizers and builders must motivate the people to the point of independence. In doing so, we revive the characteristic spirit of culture.

The importance of power building is to restore the territorial integrity of Black communities. What that does is restore public confidence in their ability to achieve completeness. Only after achieving completeness can Black people gain their independence. But first, we must revitalize Black neighborhoods, the building blocks toward nation building. That's first! Here's my perspective on the topic, for what it's worth.

Black neighborhoods, today, are broken down remnants of past communities. What that means is there aren't many, if any, Black communities existing in America today. First, a *community* is a group of people who share a common history or have similar interests existing within district areas of society. Usually, community members or residents consisted of doctors, teachers, bankers, and other notable people. These were the pillars of the community. They adhered to high moral principles or professional standards that helped to preserve community integrity. Carpenters, secretaries, janitors, mechanics, and those belonging to that group were resources. They were often parents who passed down important values to their children. They helped to give guidance on how to behave decently and honorably. Their sense of worth, importance, and usefulness added intrinsic value to the community.

Unfortunately, at one point, Black communities were flooded with crime (mid 1960's – 1970's). Measures to combat crime all but failed. In fact, crime became so pervasive in most Black communities many of the neigh-boring folk migrated out into the suburban and rural areas of the country.

Today, with most of the neighboring folk gone, all that remains are broken down neighborhoods or hoods. We've all heard the phrase, "He must be from the hood," right? A hood is the same as a shelter. It has no intrinsic value. The goodness, usefulness, or importance of that neighborhood, irrespective of the people who remain, is no longer of consequence to the person who continues to reside in it. A hood or, dare I say, hoodrat is a person who is forced to reside in urbanized areas of society even after having lost its value.

We're now working within the framework of Black cultural traditions. We're learning the languages of our people to better understand how to act upon indiscretion. Languages, though not new, are being codified—that is to say, laws, rules, and principles are being organized into signs of mutual respect—and at a time when action must be taken to avoid complete disaster or breakdown of our civil liberties. And, we are grooming neighborhood leaders who have the moral courage to hold our local politicians accountable.

Second, after each neighborhood is once again functional, we must focus on rebuilding communities. In order to rebuild a community, it must have three basic elements: There must be an independent economic structure that can produce jobs, services and goods, products, and resources for its residents. Then, it must have a code of conduct in existence. Residents must create a set of unwritten rules according to which neighboring members are supposed to adhere. That code of conduct will, in effect, be their way of behaving.

Third, the people need to elect politicians who must represent them first and foremost. These politicians must have a personal interest in residents and share the same objectives or support the same causes. They must also have an involvement with local residents that makes their progress or success important to them. This way, residents could ensure the advantages and benefits of electing politicians into office. Without those three basic elements, there can be no community, only unstable neighborhoods. Your community is a platform to power building or nation building. Without it, you cannot have sovereignty or independence.

In order to preserve the integrity of Black communities, to ensure its continued existence, its members have to practice group economics. Blacks must learn to produce, distribute, and consume goods and services well within the confines of their own community. That means they need to spend their money in their own communities. Financial spending among their own adds intrinsic value to the community, and extrinsic value to their worth. In that way, Blacks become marketable.

Second, Black people will need to forge relationships with politicians. And that's by any means necessary. The third step in the self-governing process is to convince politicians to control the judicial system to ensure community safety. The forth step is buying network media syndicates. Without controlling media outlets, Blacks cannot "communicate, organize, or motivate" their people. Fifth and last, Black people must educate themselves through formal or informal education. Education ranks last simply because you need an economy to use it. Without a structured community and stable economy, people will place little value on your education.

It may not happen when we need it to but, the time is right to rebuild that which was once lost. Black Lives Matter helped pave the way to greater competency for Blacks. Next, let's see if we can achieve a stable and just society for our people. My hope is our efforts do not go in vein.

Chapter 6
Unimpeachable: How Donald Trump Survived Being Impeached

I find hope in knowing that I belong to a state that has a lot of people who are champions of change and progress; that we will rise up and fight for justice and equality; that, ultimately, love will trump hate.

Ilhan Omar

People said Donald Trump was a narcissist. While others said he was an egoist. Does anyone remember Ethan Anthony Couch, the teenager who suffered from afluenza? Well, on June 15, 2013, in Burleson, Texas, he killed four people while driving under the influence of alcohol and drugs. If you followed his case, Trump's actions would sound eerily familiar to you.

Much like Ethan, who was not use to hearing the words no, cannot, and stop, Trump was not use to hearing people telling him what he could or could not do. In this way, he too suffered from afluenza. Yet, the only excuse Republicans attempted to make was a theory that Donald J. Trump was a victim of scrutiny. As such, they continuously refused to confront the tragic fact that Donald Trump and the Trump Administration threatened the entire Democratic process.

Trump's attempt to withhold nearly four hundred million dollars in federal aid from Ukraine, that and the conversations that took place between Trump and Ukrainian officials, ultimately led to him allegedly attempting a coup. In fact, the Trump Administration's inability to comprehend his past and present wrongdoings was what led to White House scandals. Their refusal to recognize and deal with his inappropriate behavior was what started the Democratic push into formal hearings for an impeachment against Trump.

How can a man who, by definition, lacked a certain quality of suitability befitting a US President be unimpeachable? Blurred are the principles grounded in the bylaws of a political system that should have safeguards to prevent his continued survival of impeachment. In fact, there should be no other priorities higher than the lawful sacrifice of his career.

But in America, there are no safety measures in place that, bylaw, allows a president to be impeached when he is a constant menace not only to the presidency, but the society in which he governs. Even if there is proof of wrongdoing during the time he is seated in office, apparently, a political party can step in and protect him during his period of presidency. In this way, the president is beyond reproach.

As president, Donald Trump has assumed for himself an absolute supremacy over the laws of this land. The Republican Party has stained their hands in the blood of Americans who understood Donald Trump to be a threat or danger to the American way of life. How Trump survived being impeached is a curious progression for many. Here, I offer a plausible explanation to that puzzling problem.

Unimpeachable

How Trump survived being impeached, most people will never know. One can almost say every president is impeachable with the exception of Donald Trump. Here's why! Only Congress has the power to impeach a president. Unfortunately, Congress was under the control of Republicans during Trump's presidency. That Republican controlled Congress formed a united front against Democrats, Civil Rights activists, and the citizens of America, all in support of conservatism. In failing to respond to the constitution, their constituents, public duties, and other responsibilities, Republicans have shown their unwillingness to remove Donald Trump from the Oval Office.

Some people call their willful disobedience an act of treason. They believe supporting a president who corroborates with and had long standing ties to Vladimir Putin and the Russian government was, in and of itself, an act of betrayal. Others would say he attempted to commit a coup. They would argue, as evidence, Trump and his associates begun to dismantle the US Government by first occupying the White House.

Next, they began to isolate the United States from its allies. Third, his associates began bankrupting the economy, which stems from the legacy of former President George Bush as in the great recession of 2008. Then, Trump and the Trump administration began to restructure and extend funds to expand the US Armed Forces. To expand the government in a free society, regardless of which branch, is an indication that communism is underway.

Last, he and his administration began to coordinate the mass expulsion of unwanted racial and religious groups in society, many of whom died under his watch. For many people, it appeared the Trump administration along with the Grand Old Party (GOP) and the Russian Government openly worked to bring the Western World under its dominion. And so long as Trump continued to work with Putin, there was no way Congress and the GOP would impeach him.

The problem lies well within our nation's political leaders and the oligarchy that has ruling power, authority, or control over them. Here is one of many allegations that circulated on the topic. The oligarchy wanted to reduce federal authority from the United States and its territories. Their goal was to regain then expand control over western territories. In this way, they could restore economic resources lost to free market trade industries. That gain would help them regain their status as the one percent or the cultural elite.

Respectively, a plan to dismantle the federal government would have to be put into effect decades earlier. Years of grooming would include generations assuming the duties, responsibilities, and privileges of private citizens while filtrating their way into the American infrastructure. Their job would be to form an iron-triangle comprised of policy-making relationships among congressional committees, the bureaucracy, and special interest groups. In this way, they could compete at all levels of US Government.

And in 2016, with their people in place, Republicans implemented their plan under the leadership of

Donald Trump. Trump was, quite possibly, the new face of Russia, working with a system of strategists who masqueraded themselves as a far-right network of White nationalist politicians and businessmen. Many appeared to be loyal to reviving conservatism. Most of them appeared to be committed to furthering the Republican agenda. His slogan, Make America Great Again (MAGA), was a call to restore conservatism. His plans sounded eerily close to Putin's adversarial plans to dismantle western nations, alliances, and existing powers, the very definition of a coup.

With such a debauchery taking place in the Oval Office, it would appear Trump was, in fact, impeachable. But, here's why the Democrats failed in their attempts. There were only three presidents in American history to be in jeopardy of being successfully impeached: attempts were made to impeach Andrew Johnson and Bill Clinton. Richard Nixon resigned before he could be impeached. Donald Trump was only the third president is US history who had to endure an impeachment hearing. And, he was the first to be tried in the Senate. Yet, Trump survived the hearings to continue his presidency. In fact, no sitting president has ever been successfully impeached. Thus, Donald Trump was acquitted.

The United States Constitution only gives the House of Representatives legal authority to bring formal charges of impeachment against a sitting president. It takes half of Congress to successfully process existing charges. Only the Senate has the power to bring a president to trial for impeachment. Two-thirds of the Senate must elect to convict and remove a president from office if he or she is to be successfully impeached.

Since Republicans have control of both the Senate and Judiciary, there was no chance its members would break ranks in order to impeach Trump. And it was a scary process to watch the Republican Party align themselves in support of Donald Trump during the impeachment hearings. Both parties understood his last actions were in direct violation of his solemn oath as Commander-in-Chief.

What's sad about the Democratic Party was the numerous opportunities its members had to bring an end to the GOP's domination; yet, they did nothing. Though, their failure was in no way a mistake. Democratic politicians like Hillary R. Clinton, who masqueraded as a progressive, worked to restore conservatism in the Democratic Party. What she referred to as social change in America's thinking strategy was nothing more than her willingness to preserve the status quo in favor of protecting traditional values and customs.

The need to restore conservatism as part of the Democratic process is rooted in the key role that the Conservative Coalition once played in controlling Congress. In the past, during the 1930's to early 1960's, conservatism was the lifestyle for Democrats throughout the country but especially in the Southern United States.

Since the mid 1960's, however, the country began to see a shift in party affiliations. For example, Republicans in the United States would begin to support political views that endorsed the existing state of society as worthy of preservation. They became unwilling or slow to accept change or new ideas and began to preserve the status quo. That dynamic shift in party affiliation may very well have been step one in the dismantling of our political process. The only concern with politicians and their Post-Party Conservative movement is their alleged coup attempt was, perhaps, the first of many more close encounters with communism to come.

A Sad Performance

The saddest performance at Trump's impeachment hearings was not of Republicans portraying him as a victim in an underhanded attempt to control the outcome. However, it did show how the Republican Party had the intention to secretively and dishonestly deceive the American people. Rather, what's sad was how the Democrats performed in front of America as if a successful impeachment was possible. They understood long before going into the hearings Donald Trump could not be impeached without the full on cooperation of the Republican Party—a sad fact that spoke begrudgingly to Democrats and their loss of Congressional control caused by power-sharing with oppressed sects of government.

The loss of Congressional control became evident during the presidential election of 2016 when Donald J. Trump was elected into the Oval Office as America's forty-fifth US President. Most Americans were caught off guard since the overwhelming majority voted for Hillary Clinton. America felt betrayed as the Electoral College turned against the popular vote only to favor Donald Trump and the Republican Party. Truly, Trump was not the best qualified candidate to elect into the Oval Office. What's worst were Democratic voters felt like the Electoral College betrayed Democracy.

In this way, voters felt the move to elect Trump was welcomed by members of both parties. Eight years of Obama as President and the possibility of Hillary Clinton being seated for, potentially, another eight years scared Electoral members more than the Republican Party. The point is not so much about our White political leaders fearing the loss of their country to minorities in their quest for change, which they did. The point here is a man who was the first Black President of America managed to bridge the gap between Whites and Blacks, dismiss cultural stereotypes about Black people, forged unshakable unions between religions, and knocked down racial barriers during the eight years he spent in office. Eight years was more than enough for our White political leaders to betray their oath of office so they could rebuild conservatism in America.

Hence, the majority decision to elect an unqualified candidate as America's forth-fifth US President. Certainly, after what they felt was the smoke clearing, a few members admitted to Trump's mediocrity by comparing it to Bush's mediocrity as if mediocrity was no justification to remove a seated president from the Oval Office. However, and most unfortunate, it did pave the way for more unqualified candidates to run a political campaign in future elections.

How did the Electoral College manage to succumb to betrayal? Why did the Republican strategy win the Electoral College? First, Trump's appeal to the public—he claimed to care about working class citizens who lived in Middle America. They were being overlooked by the US Government as their factories were being closed down. Many of his supporters voted for the first time, ever. Along with his openness and seemingly genuine concern for their wellness, Trump promised to restore the nation to greatness. Second, Trump did not appear to be interested in playing politics more than he was willing to conduct big business to help restore the economy. The American economy was still in a tremendous crisis at the time, working class citizens were struggling, and many middleclass citizens were adding to the homeless crisis.

In contrast, Hillary Clinton had much of Black America duped by codifying her speeches. Her speeches appealed to the masses. But, each one was crafted to persuade conservatives to come back to the Democratic Party. Conservative White Americans left the Democratic Party years earlier. Those former Democrats left the party for more assurance that the White race would continue to lead America in the twenty-first century.

Black people were surprised by Hillary's forward attempts at progressive thinking. As an advocate of social, political, or economic reforms, Hillary believed in family. She believed the government should have worked to enhance the family unit. She also sought to ensure local public assistance programs were reformed to keep families together. She fiercely fought corporate health insurance lobbyists to enact universal health coverage, which was the cornerstone of her campaign.

So why did political progressives look at Hillary with such disdain? Some say she had a deep procorporate ideology that was built on Ronald Reagan's legacy of supply-side economics, deemed Reaganomics. And as a Senator, in 2002, Hillary voted to authorize the invasion of Iraq. It was the first serious disagreement that disrupted relations with progressives and Democratic supporters. Next, she distanced herself from anti-war voters by criticizing President Barack Obama for pledging to meet with leaders of oppressed countries during his first year in office. She responded with a rhetorical answer in conversation about whether undocumented immigrants should receive driver's licenses. When criminal mischief and embezzling in Wall Street nearly bankrupted the global economy, Bill Clinton's deregulation policies quickly became the subject of heated political and scholarly debate, and Hillary's ties to the financial industry were scrutinized. Along with her lack of ties to the Black community, in 2016, Hillary simply fell short with progressives and in establishing herself as a voice for the people.

Unfortunately, the very nature of Trump's inappropriate behavior did not qualify as grounds for disqualification. Yet, so long as conservatism governed his thoughts and actions, Donald Trump would continue to receive endorsements from conservatives in both political parties—as Republicans and other conservatives sit back and reap the benefits of building a dominant White society.

How do we undermine conservatism when it underlined most people's reasoning?

We must slowly and methodically dismantle its foundation. The basic goal of undermining and dismantling conservatism is to replace it with progressivism, to understand that progressive thinking is not a love affair with liberalism or socialism. Rather, it is a plan to reform our social, economical, and political systems gradually and in a way that change does not occur abruptly but over a period of time. The problem then becomes one of a refusal to undermine and dismantle the thinking strategies (foundation) of conservatives.

Let's talk about Trump's legitimacy as a conservative—a claim made about Trump by his constituents that did not go over so well with his party members. What is conservatism? Who is conservative, really? First, conservatism is a misunderstood term. It has no place in life outside the political philosophy and practice of politics. In fact, when most people use the word conservative, they're referring to reserved or restrained and mindful—whereas conservatism is a right-of-center political philosophy based on a tendency to support gradual rather than abrupt change and to preserve the status quo.

Most politicians who do believe in conservatism tend to have an aversion to change and thus avoid any and all possibility of liberalism, socialism, and progressivism. Yet, how the word is defined in politics and used largely in society varies. Any claims to conservatism—beyond being a byproduct of an ideology that views the current state of affairs as worthy of preservation and being an heir to the grand tradition of White supremacy—is contingent on one's political definition of Republicanism and one's general understanding of progressiveness in and outside the community of life.

In short, conservatism is a political construct. Appeals to Democratic conservatism embrace this point: conservatism hides and conceals a political agenda that opts to reestablish White supremacy. This claim is the reason why legitimate conservatism outweighs progressivism—or why conservatism tends to dominate over progressivism. Every claim of legitimate conservatism is an agreement to show an attitude of condescension toward strangers and others in politics and in society.

Conservatism conceals such attitudes behind a deception of consciousness. Yet, conservatism is popularized or, even, romanticized due to its illegitimate acts of kindness associated with the Republican claim that President Abraham Lincoln emancipated slaves during the Civil War (1865). Such illegitimacy is the reason why the public's claim to Trump's legitimacy as a conservative, Trump's claim about his own legitimacy, and the Republican claim to legitimate conservatism highlights a history of violence toward Blacks, Hispanics, minorities, strangers, and others.

But if claims to legitimate conservatism are measurements of a relationship that exist between Democrats and Republicans, then any attempt to confront claims of legitimate conservatism among Republicans or Democrats warrants suspicion. For example, Trump claimed that automotive company owners who took their business overseas to profit were taking away from working class citizens. That he would bring automotive companies back home to Middle America was the type of empty rhetoric that revealed his own lack of integrity and character. But the failure by Democrats to highlight the nature of this shortcoming is a measure of the bipartisan relationship that exists between conservative Republicans and their conservative Democratic counterparts. In short, the refusal of most conservative Democrats to give weight to his shortcomings was already apparent among conservative Republicans.

Claims to legitimate conservatism, which characterizes social exclusion, are dangerous precisely because it's usually done at the expense or consideration of Black people. It also tends to ignore divisions of class in society—divisions that should be given attention if Black communities are to be taken seriously. Trump's conservative policies were very exclusionary. He claimed legitimate conservatism to promote his own ambitions, that is to say, to gain in prestige and power. Early in his life, Trump was a Democrat. During that time, he did not appear to be influenced by moncy or power. But, as a Republican and business professional, the rest of his life surrounded wealth, power, and income. He also began promoting individual achievement and race-free merit systems. Yet, when his popularity declined with Republicans in the younger generation and in the opinion polls, he became real friendly with Black figures and entertainers like Kanye West and Kim Kardashian to gain more support and build momentum for his personal gains. And, it was most unfortunate that Trump managed to take advantage of so many Black Americans who legitimately believed he was sincere about their wellness.

Trump played Black Americans brilliantly, first by appealing to their safety or wellness, and then to his victimization as a misunderstood politician new to the game—primarily because of a deep culture of conservatism that exist in both White and Black communities. In White communities, conservatism takes on the social role of social exclusion and persecution. Hence, they are only willing to work with Black people who are ready and willing to follow their orders, instructions, or requests, typically in a way considered overly slavish.

In Black communities, conservatism takes on the xenophobic roles of aversion (i.e. avoidance of strangers and others) and internalized racism (hatred of people from one's own race). Like any form of conservatism, be it White, Black, cultural, et cetera, it focuses in on the most neglected and downtrodden members of the community. For White conservatives, it means they will displace their aggressions onto Blacks, Hispanics, stranger, and others while they attempt to shamefully hide or shield their poor or downtrodden from exploitation of others.

For Black conservatives, it means they will distance themselves from poor Black people often while assuming the role of victim. In this way, both Whites and Blacks who lay legitimate claims to conservatism, reinforce the prejudice associated with White supremacy and American racism. Until the election of Donald Trump, these claims could not be substantiated, only speculated. It also showed how conservatism led to indifference between Republicans and Democrats in American politics. That is to say, neither parties feel a sense of compassion for politicians who are not a part of their political philosophy.

Impeachment Hearings

Trump made a not so unexpected decision when he refused to participate in the impeachment hearings. Instead, he counterattacked the House of Representatives by relying on his allies to not just acquit him but seek out political retribution. Trump was charged with two articles of impeachment: abuse of power and obstructing Congress, accusations he felt were unfair. The House gave President Trump a fair opportunity to question witnesses and present his own argument to address the overwhelming evidence before the US House Committee on the Judiciary. But having declined his opportunity, Trump could not claim the process to be unfair.

Outside the hearings, images that emerged of Donald Trump were favorable. Republican supporters viewed the impeachment hearings as a witch hunt. They claimed Democrats were in the practice of using unsubstantiated accusations to discredit President Trump. Others, more extreme, said the Democrats were deeply engaged in a *McCarthyism*—the practice of publicly accusing the president of Communist activities or sympathies, especially without having real evidence to substantiate their claims.

Religious supporters saw Trump as a messiah who would restore America back to a time when Whites were sure of themselves by reestablishing world order. Others viewed Trump simply as a patriot engaged in a never-ending battle for truth, justice, and the American way, American way being White-only.

Collectively, they viewed Trump as a liberator of America, White people and, quite possibly, the world. There should also be little doubt that Trump's decision not to testify was a calculated move to appeal to the masses. Many people said Donald Trump was calculated in every move he made. For me, it seemed he usually operated with limited knowledge and/or concern for consequences. Why? Trump's tweeting about the justice department disrupted the nature of his relationship with Attorney General William P. Barr. How callous he must be to continue tweeting about the justice department while Barr was in the middle of investigating members involved in the Russia probe, an investigation that once threatened his presidency. You have to wonder whether Barr viewed Trump in the same light as when they first encountered each other.

Truth be told, progressivism would have liberated conservative Democrats. To embrace progressivism would enable them to remove any guilt from feeling obligated to support Trump especially since he was unqualified to hold the title of Commander-in-Chief. Much like supporters of the popular vote, politicians from both political parties could have opposed Trump and with the comfort of knowing he was totally unqualified and unprincipled. And party members could have chosen a more formidable opponent in Hillary Clinton. Conservatives from both political parties could have avoided being duped by Trump's broken promises, his empty rhetoric, and vulgar appeals to Republicans, most of whom wanted him acquitted. Unlike supporters of the popular vote, who saw past Trump's shenanigans, conservatives could have called him out as they saw him: as a menace to society.

Unfortunately, many Democrats remained caught in the grasp of conservatism, even when they opposed Trump and favored Hillary Clinton—just like ninety-seven percent of the Black community who were duped into voting for her—even though she too was a conservative masquerading as a progressive. Rarely do we have a Democratic leader who underscores the importance of progressivism as part of the Democratic process. Rarely does he or she have a need to advocate for social reform, or appeal to the public's trust in the name of justice.

Instead, what we had was a growing coalition of strategists who followed behind xenophobic conservatives in the Republican Party —a right-of-center political faction with existing members who historically oppressed women and minorities after claiming they supported equality for everyone.

In supporting a political party with members whose tendency is to preserve the status quo—not just for the sake of caution but due to their fear of change—Democrats once again missed out on a grand opportunity to have deep intellectual discussions about race in America.

We know there's no depending on Republicans to have that discussion, the big talk. So long as Democrats allow their members to be completely controlled by conservatism, they will forever be manipulated by public oratory like Trump's empty rhetoric which is how his blatant language managed to increase killings by cops among young Black Americans, like the influence he had on domestic terrorism in America, and just like the power he had to award the Medal of Freedom—the highest civilian honor the nation has to offer—to a blatant racist like Rush Limbaugh. The sad fact is people will be excluded from what's important in life without a voice or true political representative who shares the same beliefs as the people who elected him or her. They will be just another burden our government is unwilling to give due attention to. Then we become people who are not important enough to consider and so not worth worrying about. In this way, the system has no problem excluding us from fully participating in the Democratic process.

The thuggish mentality of Donald Trump results, in part, from the violent history of racism that ties him to conservatism we see in the White House. If this notion is true, and he still was unimpeachable, then how Trump survived being impeached is a true testament to their unwillingness or slowness to accept what is right, fair, or just. In this way, the Mike Pence's, the David Duke's, and the Rush Limbaugh's of American racism—who strongly desire to preserve current societal structures—are clearly better suited to be seated in the Oval Office. And Mike Pence, Trump's number one crony, just may get that chance. Unfortunately, the current state of Republicanism does not reflect the bureaucratic process we call democracy.

However, there are those willing to forward our cause. They believe that the people (the citizens of America) should have control of our government—and, should have free and equal rights to participate in decision-making processes—especially any decision-making having to do with a demoralized and exploited people like Black Americans. Anyone who has the humanity or decency to care should take these words into consideration. And, many more should continue practicing in this way if we are to truly become a democracy.

Chapter 7
An Act of Charity: Should Blacks Receive Reparations

Overcoming poverty is not a gesture of charity. It is an act of
justice.

Nelson Mandela (1918 – 2013)

Should Blacks receive reparations? It's becoming a historical argument. Perhaps, it's part of a tactic? Maybe Blacks are using reparations as some charitable event to uplift themselves from poverty?

Nelson Mandela (1918 – 2013) once said, "Overcoming poverty is not a gesture of charity. It is an act of justice." If it takes giving an added advantage or opportunity to those who would otherwise be at a disadvantage—or by attempting to take away or diminish advantages from dominant society just to make their situation fair or just—then let reparations be a fitting means to a heinous end. For Black people, anything less would be an act of charity. In this chapter, we will take a look at whether the United States should compensate American Descendants of Slaves.

Black people feel that the avoidance of conversation on reparations is a political tactic. The idea is if the conversation is avoided for a prolonged period of time then, perhaps, it could be proven slavery happened too long ago for anyone to do anything about it. We do know official slavery occurred in 1619. That's over four hundred years ago! However, physical slavery ended after the Civil War (1865). But, its violent past would haunt America throughout its history.

Since slavery's official end, America bore witnessed to Jim Crow segregation, the eugenics movements, the Civil Rights movement, along with prejudice and discrimination well into the new millennium. Regardless of how long ago it happened, American Descendents of Slaves (#ADOS) continue to have their lives impacted or disrupted. But slavery is such a hot button issue, it brings up other emotionally charged disputes we cannot seem to settle: racism, confederate statues and, yes, reparations.

Should the United States compensate American Descendents of Slaves? The idea was not so long ago thought to be radical. But, recently, the idea was mainstreamed, like integration, interracial marriage, and Affirmative Action. There are some naysayers, at large, expressing contrary opinions over reparations. But, the question still remains.

After the Civil War ended (1865), Union General William Sherman issued special field orders that established provisions not to succeed more than forty acres of land and a mule to freed slaves. It was made available by the acts of war and in a proclamation made by US President Abraham Lincoln. Unfortunately, the act was carried out but for only four to five months. After the assassination of President Lincoln, newly appointed President Andrew Johnson ordered all land areas to be returned to former slave holders. There were components of the Freedman Bureau Act and the Southern Home Stead Act that had similar types of distributions set aside for freed slaves. However, orders were rescinded.

Although he was a member of the union, Andrew Johnson was antiblack or had a proslavery disposition. As a result, he refused to honor President Lincoln's proclamation; thus, Lincoln's orders were never carried out. So, the debate for reparations has been ongoing for more than one hundred fifty-five years, since Jim Crow segregation was introduced to the south.

After the Civil War (1865), racial segregation was introduced to the American south. The slave codes or Jim Crow laws were a national decree that enforced racial segregation, especially by enforcing the use of separate schools, transportation, housing, and other facilities for Blacks. It was often used to discriminate against Black people in the Southern United States. That's not to say racial segregation never existed in Northern States. Actually, it existed in the North from 1809, starting with the first five free slave states. The decree became federal law after the Reconstruction period. The laws were enforced until 1965. It is the duty of this country—and every country that participated in the Trans-Atlantic Slave Trade—to reimburse American descendents of slaves.

What Role Did Segregation Play?

Segregation played an extremely gruesome role in the justification of reparations. It lasted in America for most of the twentieth century. It was a social caste system stratified by class. The hierarchy was meant to prevent Whites and Blacks from coming into contact with each other. Segregation was the lifestyle for Blacks throughout the country but especially in the Southern United States.

The White man had the official rule of law during segregation; and, if southern Blacks failed to acknowledge him, did not yield right of way to him, or looked too long at a White woman, they could be subjected to punishment, often by way of death. The Ku Klux Klan—a terrorist group and secret society organized in the South after the Civil War—was one of a few factions that used violence and murder to intimidate Black people.

But, there were always Blacks who fought against segregation. For example, the Black church stood against inequality. And, with the help of Black unions and organizations like the National Association for the Advancement of Colored People (NAACP), they worked decades for equality through protest, speeches, demonstrations, and court cases.

World War II had a profound impact on Black people and their quest for change. They were segregated into military units that were kept apart from White units. And for the duration of the war, they fought and died in segregated units. Blacks developed a new way of thinking as some were trained in leadership roles, others as specialists in their units. This change invigorated their hope that with new identities would come new opportunities for everyone regardless of race, ethnicity, religion, gender, or social class. Many were waiting to become accepted members of society and their status as military war heroes would give them the courage to stand up and do it.

Unfortunately, the South wasn't ready to hear Negro demands for change. Neither was the nation ready to talk about integration. Then it happened, sometime in the early 1950's. After years of planning and taking careful measures, the NAACP brought a list of policy demands before the Supreme Court. The demands were based on test cases conducted in grade schools. And, on May 17, 1954, the Supreme Court decided unanimously against segregation in the ruling of Brown vs. the Board of Education, stating that segregated schools were unconstitutional. It raised doubt about the entire system of segregation. It would be years before the ruling was implemented. But, one thing did happen that would set the tone for the Civil Rights movement. Emit Till's body would be found at the bottom of the Tallahatchie River in Tennessee on September of 1955. Why? He allegedly talked fresh to a White woman.

Attempts to reconcile the situation were futile. Other attempts in places like Mississippi would be met with pushback. Black people's efforts to overcome segregation were too few and too soon. Then, months later in Montgomery, Alabama, many Black people came together and started the movement every Black person was awaiting. The Montgomery, Alabama bus boycott began. And it began after Rosa Parks refused to accommodate a White person.

In Alabama, life was segregated. There were white-only policies in place that included White-only water fountains, White-only restaurants, housing, even bus systems were segregated. If Blacks rode the bus, they could only ride in the back. If a seat was needed for a White person, a Black person would have to give up the seat. Police were used to aid in enforcing the laws of segregation.

On December 1, 1955, while riding the metro bus service, Rosa Park refused to offer her seat to a White person. Ms. Parks, a twelve year member of the NAACP and rebel to the cause was arrested and charged for failure to adhere to a lawful order. She was bailed out on one hundred dollars fine. E.D. Nixon, the president of the NAACP, with Ms. Parks permission, called for a one day bus boycott, which turned out to be a success.

Later on that evening, a community of Blacks rallied at the Holt Street Baptist Church for a meeting. It was decided that evening to continue the boycott. That evening, Dr. Martin Luther King, Jr., community organizers, leading members of Civil Rights organizations, and other Organizational leaders started what could only be the largest Civil Rights movement ever witnessed. The rest is history.

In brief, reparations for slavery are merely a compensation not only for past wrongdoings, but also because White people continue to wrong Blacks in order to achieve long lasting negative effects on them and their children.

Why Should Institutions Pay?

Why should institutions pay out reparations for a country's past sins? Many institutions benefited from the eugenics movement to include psychiatry, the judicial system, our political system, along with colleges and universities.

Eugenics, though it had not yet been officially named, was well underway in the 1800's. James Marion Sims or, sometimes, J. Marion Sims (1813 – 1883) —as I believed he preferred his middle name—is known as the father of modern gynecology. He was an American physician and a pioneer in the field of surgery. Perhaps, his greatest contribution to medicine was the development of laparoscopic surgery, a surgical technique used in the repair of vesicovaginal fistula, an unwanted opening that forms between the bladder and the wall of the vagina. What a great surgical technique, right? Perhaps!

Sims used enslaved African women as medical experimental research subjects (M.E.R.S.) to perfect his technique. Countless African women died (i.e., were ripped apart) in what could only be called trial and error surgery. You would be happy to know that every surgery took place without the use of anesthesia. That's right, not only modern medicine but American society benefited from slavery. Indeed, it did!

Perhaps the greatest contributor of slavery was one of the most productive slave owners in America. John Hoskins of Baltimore, Maryland was a medical physician who owned more than ten thousand slaves. He used slaves to teach medical ethics to his students. John Hoskins had a medical school named after him. Unfortunately, the fictitious name Hopkins was invented in order to hide his fiendish deeds. Today, the medical institution is called Johns Hopkins University.

Later support for the Civil Rights movement came from the Supreme Court after learning undesirable traits could be passed down genetically. Sir Francis Galton—incidentally, half-cousin to Charles Darwin, the father of evolution—coined the term eugenics in the late 1800's. He applied the principles of genetics and heredity for the purpose of improving the White race. Eugenics was not only consumed by academics, it became a popular social movement at the height of the Great Depression.

The American Eugenics Society was a social movement geared toward the proposed improvement of the human species by encouraging or permitting reproduction of only those people with genetic characteristics judged desirable. It, along with dominant society, eventually reaped the benefits of exploitation and extreme sacrifices made by countless minorities, most of whom were descendants of slaves, many more judged undesirable. And although the eugenics movement officially ended in 1975—it has been regarded with disfavor—but not before assuming responsibility for the forced sterilization of over sixty-four thousand people in the United States. If reparations cannot be established on historical grounds, along with the case of eugenics, it should rest solely on ethics.

The eugenics movement was chronicled in a book entitled Medical Apartheid: The Dark History of Medical Experimentation on Black Americans from Colonial Times to the Present, written by authors Harriet A. Washington, Ron Butler, et al.

Why Should Today's Society Pay

Today's society should pay out reparations since its dark history continues. The United States has taken a dark path to continue its violent history. Its more obvious path includes racial prejudice and discrimination. In the new millennium, racism is becoming more overt. As a result, Black Americans have more problems claiming reparations than Jewish and Japanese Americans.

Today, dominant society appears less in tuned to the needs of Black Americans then it was just two decades earlier. Still, many White folk continue to support Black people's rights to acquire reparations. Why? Violence by Whites toward Blacks has increased considerably. For example, White police abuse and domestic terrorism continue to increase. There is also growing resistance to programs that would help Black people reach full equality, programs like Affirmative Action and school desegregation. The idea that conservatives are willing to adopt liberal racial attitudes has shifted to them resisting further change. Conservatives are no longer supporting integration; and, that's a fact. They are blatant in their position on racial inequality. They also understand their decision not to support integration has costly implementation. In fact, today's Whites are more comfortable supporting conservatism and at the expense or consideration of Black people.

At one point in time, conservatives appeared to sympathize with Blacks but blamed them for their personal failings. However, the days of subtle racism are gone. Their discomfort, uneasiness, and fear are losing its hold on them. Many conservatives are now emboldened to use prejudice and discrimination to reflect hostility and hatred toward Blacks. Not too long ago, conservatives simply avoided Blacks, perhaps, due to the shame they experienced from holding animosity toward them. Today, the subtlety implied in their demeanor is nothing more than a cliché.

With Donald Trump and his administration representing the Republican Party, and Republicans having control in both the judiciary and the Senate, the feeling of subtlety has lost its original effectiveness or power over them. In this way, the debate over reparations will continue.

The Arc of Justice:
Advocates of Reparations

Many people on both sides argue the pros and cons of reparations. Advocates, who are in favor of reparations, call it the Arc of Justice. They recognize or acknowledge the idea that reparations should be redressed in order to bring about closure. Here's a shared response for what it's worth.

They acknowledge there has been an egregious social injustice committed against Black Americans. In order to impose fairness on those who have been repeatedly wronged throughout America's intellectual history, Whites should adjust their situation to make life experiences fair, equal, or just in society. In that way, America can lay down its sin of blood. Certainly, it doesn't mean we as a nation should or would completely forget the topic of slavery. What closure does mean is Americans could finally have an open-ended discussion on a topic once thought to be forbidden.

America should make amends for the wrong that is being done to Black people. But, therein lies the problem. We say Americans are haunted by the reality of racism. When, in effect, most are ill at ease by unpleasant reminders that they fear losing their place in society. The problem is that many people in dominant society continue to harbor racist feelings toward Black people. In fact, many are willing to perpetuate racism opposed to promoting peace. We say they are addicted to racial violence.

For example, a Black person is abused or even murdered by a White police officer and the situation did not call for it. Also, White people in Virginia called for a civil war just because a new gun bill proposed a stricter registration process to purchase fire arms. These incidents have nothing to do with haunted feelings or a daunting reality. It has more to do with the changing face of racism, which seems to have replaced the old-fashioned forms. Subtle and subversive forms of racism make it hard to bring an end to discrimination.

The understanding is Blacks need to experience some sense of finality in coming to terms with hostilities endured not only from being American Descendents of Slaves but because of their low socioeconomic status in America as felt or experienced over time. In this way, reparations are a means to provide compensation for damages committed to a people who experienced loss or have been consistently wronged throughout their intellectual history. And if not, at least, acknowledged, compensation should continue to be demanded by Black people for a war America is ultimately responsible for, especially as demanded of General William Sherman by the proclamation of President Lincoln after the Civil War.

Critics of Reparations

Critics contradict optimists with opposing arguments. They appear confused about exactly who should receive reparations and how it should or if it could ever be fairly distributed among its rightful descendents. They believe the idea of handing out reparations to Black people is unfair to the average American. And, they question the effects it would have on Americans whose descendents had nothing to do with slavery.

When an immigrant moves to a new country and settles there, she or he reaps the benefits of all the labor or hard work that came before. That person also benefits from an injection of new ideas. Along with receiving benefits, it is customary to assume the duties, morals, and responsibilities of that country. It is often expected of the newcomer to support the country if called upon and to preserve or even protect its way of life. It is, in part, the process of being a citizen. Other critics who oppose reparation argue the time has long since passed. That American Descendents of Slaves no longer have a right to claim reparations.

Unfortunately, what critics fail to realize is the injustices of slavery was not so long ago. When viewed in generational terms, we begin to see its continuation. That is to say, we see various dimensions of slavery appear after it supposedly ended. That's why the quest for reparations involves not only US slavery, but Jim Crow segregation—which lasted 100 years after it was introduced to the south—the eugenics movements in which case the government reinstituted segregation, and then sterilized Blacks thought to be inferior. They also conducted illegal experiments on generations of Black people with lasting effects reaching well into the new millennium.

Then there's the perpetually thorny problem of racism, which continues on today. Each of these recurring problems greatly contribute to America's outstanding obligations to American Descendents of Slaves. So, it's not just the question of reparations for slavery, but atonement for Jim Crow segregation and the ongoing discrimination of Black folk in American society.

Still, more critics would argue that reparations for Blacks are a public handout. They feel Black people need to achieve success by their own efforts. Black people should learn how to pull themselves up by the bootstraps since they're starting from very difficult circumstances. They believe it should be done without help from anyone just like the immigrants of Europe a few generations earlier.

What critics fail to realize is that the majority of European immigrants who sought refuge in America arrived with their families in tacked. Most had full government support, many later in the form of public assistance. In contrast, Black people's situation comes from having lost cultural and psychological contact with both their traditional society and the larger dominant society. Slavery, segregation, poverty, discrimination, and poor education document the impact of their living conditions. Many, disorganized and unsupportive, are said to suffer from severe stress and oppression. Such conditions lead Whites to believe Black Americans lack ambition.

Even so, there is no such thing as a merit-based system in America, not even with the induction of Affirmative Action. At one point or another, people receive a helping hand from the next person. For example, an employer opens up the door to opportunity for you. Yes, that employer gave you a hand, perhaps, in exchange for the work you're willing to do. But, more importantly, that employer hired a person "in need" of employment. That, by definition, is the spirit of charity.

As for the critics who speak on public handouts as charity, there will always be an exchange between parties in the spirit of cooperation. Just remember, there is always something asked in return whenever someone gives out a hand. So, there should be caution not rejoice noted whenever people discuss charity.

Who Should Receive Reparations?

With regard to who would be eligible for reparations, the only people who should receive funding are those who can provide documentation proving they descend from slavery or their ancestry dates back to the period of US slavery. Blacks or those claiming American ancestry would also be required to prove they were registered within the last ten years as Black or African American with the US Censor Bureau.

In terms of dollar amount, various research groups estimated the cost accumulated through slavery as nine point twelve billion dollars, plus an annual interest rate of five percent dating back to 1865 until present. Other estimates for reparations range from four trillion dollars—whereby many Black people say that is a very conservative estimate—to sixty-five trillion dollars, which for many Whites, doesn't seem realistic.

But, realistically, sixty-five trillion dollars in reparations is quite workable. If the government breaks up the total cost into dividends or monthly payments paid out over the course of the lifespan, it would offset any financial strains the government may acquire. Other spending for reparations could also include trust funds, building and business development programs, educational program and opportunities, et cetera. And let's not forget land (40 acres) and the implements (the mule). There are a variety of ways reparations can be distributed. There's nothing that commits us to having a reparations program that takes on a single form.

For example, there are a few models that could be used to outline a reparations program. One such model is a compensation for war program in which there would be compensation demanded of a defeated nation (like the US Confederacy) by the victor in a war (the Union), much like what was demanded of Germany by the Treaty of Versailles after World War I.

Holocaust survivors were also given reparations at the modest sum of five hundred dollars a month for the remainder of their lives. Today, the descendents of the holocaust survivors receive the remainder of reparations as part of a treaty agreement reached after World War II. Even Israel was given reparations to assist in its continued existence. So, we could have some form of institution building that takes place as a result of the overall reparations program. We should be optimistic about reparations so long as it has the constructive goal of closing the disparity that exists between Whites and Blacks in American society.

Last, there are those critics who believe America would bankrupt itself if Blacks receive reparations.

The annual budget for the nation is more than six trillion dollars. Reparations, spread out over the course of a lifespan, are certainly doable. Remember, the government does not have to pull resources from its annual budget. A Chicago Judge, Robin Rue Simmons, may have already laid the blueprint for funding reparations. She used funding that will be taken from the sales taxes of recreational marijuana use. What a good idea, right?

There are numerous ways to approach reparation funding for Black Americans. But, the government must first be willing to consider it. Again, if the government considers implementing programs geared toward revitalization and planning, urban renewal, trust funds, education, building and business opportunities, land and home owner-ship, et cetera, it is most certainly doable.

Unfortunately, there are critics in the Black community who are skeptical about reparations for Black folk. They feel it is an unrealistic task. That reparation for Blacks cannot be achieved under the current state of society. Many also feel there is a creditability issue at risk. That under the current system, organizations that endorse or support the quest for reparations will no longer be taken seriously.

Be it morally correct or correct policy-wise, there were many bills proposed we never thought would work out. We were wrong about Affirmative Action, integration, civil unions, and more. Yet, each proposal helped to build America by adding strength and character to its integrity. So, reparations could make their situation fair and balanced. It is hopeful those organizations will come to support reparations for American Descendents of Slaves.

We have not been able to bring an end to racism and bigotry in the absence of a reparations program. For now, the best we can do is continue to have open discussions on the topic. It will help people understand that reparations for Black people are not an absurdity. That it is a way to shed light on the violent history of racism in America. And, it is a way for us to confront our ugly xenophobic resentment so we can bring about closure to race matters in America.

Epilogue
The Changing Face of Politics

As we are captivated by the energies of the twenty-first century, the face of politics is already changing in our nation's capital. We are currently experiencing the early development of cultural diversity. So far, we experienced diversity in the freshman class of Congresswomen, more of them racial minority members than in previous times. A larger number of minority women will enter politics, putting greater pressure on society to help balance the demands of working class and poor families.

Americans argue that their bureaucratic system is failing and at a noticeable rate. Sadly, no one in past administrations was willing to cooperate with Democrats to hash out a strategy to better our situation. The Trump administration was working with increasing regularity to restore the violent legacy of America's past. And while more minimum wage jobs were being developed at an increasing rate, the middle-class was being reduced in numbers, and more or new affluent jobs had yet to be made available to save a once flourishing and promising community. As a result, the success of many politicians may rest on the ability to relate to working class citizens, even the poor.

It is becoming increasingly complex and more demanding to become a politician. As the country changes, conservatism will begin to take a back seat in its role on influencing the nation. As the way of conservatism becomes obsolete, and due to the changing demographic tapestry of culture, it will require considerable thought and influencing to elicit support.

Many citizens are dependent on jobs to sustain and maintain a healthy lifestyle. As a result, our nation's leaders are realizing that employment is an important topic for promoting a campaign. Many politicians developed agendas to help the working class improve their situation. Yet, no one has an agenda to help change the situation of Black folk and the poor.

Since we live in a complex, rapidly changing, multicultural world, there is a special sense of urgency in developing a political agenda for minorities. Due to changes in the population makeup, by 2035, non-Hispanic whites will be outnumbered by minorities. Between the years 2000 and 2010, Hispanics had the largest population increase, growing by 15.2 million people or 43 percent. Black and Asian populations each increased by more than 4 million, with growth rates of 12.3 percent and 43.3 percent, respectively. The multiracial American growth rate increased from 1.4 percent to 2.9 percent of the population from 1990 to 2010. Today, they represent the fastest-growing population (45.9 percent) under age 18. Three important tasks politicians might like to consider are:

1. Research and knowledge development of growth rates for minority population groups
2. To develop a better understanding of behavior that apply to diverse minority groups
3. To develop wellness programs that promote healthcare, immigration, and public education reform

What are important minority issues that require political attention? They include the following:

1. Understanding diversity among racial, ethnic, cultural, and gender identity groups
2. Recognizing and respecting legitimate differences among racial, ethnic, cultural, and gender identity groups
3. Search for similarities among racial, ethnic, cultural, and gender identity groups before differences are incorrectly assumed.
4. Developing better ways to reduce discrimination and prejudice
5. Understanding that value conflicts are often important factors in resolving problems among racial and ethnic identity groups
6. Developing a global understanding of politics while learning that the American political system is greatly ethnocentric
7. Recognizing or acknowledging that behavior is not the result of a single process to include criminal behavior. That wellness should be promoted through psychological intervention
8. Considering different viewpoints on problems of various racial, ethnic, and gender identity groups
9. Using politics to promote and improve minority-based problems and recognizing minority issues as mainstream concerns

References

Alexander, M. (2015). <u>Black Lives Matter</u>. Social Media [Online] Available: https://www.facebook.com/pages/Michelle-Alexander/168304409924191

Alexander, M. (2012). <u>The New Jim Crow: Mass Incarceration in the Age of Colorblindness</u>. New York, NY.The New Press

Allen, L. & Santrock, J. W. (1993). <u>Psychology: The Context of Behavior</u>. Dubuque, Iowa. Wm. Brown Communications, Inc.

Anderson, C. (2018). White Rage: The Unspoken Truth of Our Nation's Divide. Social Media. [Online] Available: https://www.youtube.com/watch?v=YBYUET24K1c

Anderson, C. (2019). Dr. Claud Anderson Discusses America's Race Based Society, PowerNomics + More. The Breakfast Club Power 105.1. [Online] Available: https://www.youtube.com/watch?v=fW39KOf_f04&t=3571s

Anonymous. (2020). Oligarchy. Search Engine. [Online] Available: www.google.com

Bradley, M. (1978). <u>The Iceman Inheritance: Prehistoric Sources of Western Man's Racism, Sexism and Aggression</u>. New York, NY: Kayode Publications LTD

Clinton, H. R. (2019). <u>All Lives Matter</u>. Social Media [Online] Available: https://www.youtube.com/results?search_query=all+lives+matter

Darity, W. A. (2009). <u>Black Reparations</u>. Social Media. [Online] Available: https://www.youtube.com/watch?v=z84nFEYh4Ck

Darity, W. A. (2016). <u>Wealth and Structural Racism</u>.

[Online] Available: https://www.youtube.com/watch?v=W-cQBOd-3VQ

Darity, W. A. (2020). <u>The Arc of Justice: Reparations for African Americans</u>. Can TV [Online] Available: https://www.youtube.com/watch?v=s3mSCwOIBjU

Documentary (2016). <u>Eyes On The Prize (Part 1)</u>: Awakenings 1954-1956 Americas Civil Rights Movement. [Online] Available: https://www.youtube.com/watch?v=NpY2NVcO17U

Documentary (2019). <u>Black Lives Matter</u>. Social Media

[Online] Available:
https://www.youtube.com/results?search_query=bla
ck+lives+matter

Documentary (2019). <u>Can Reparations Help Right the
Wrongs of Slavery</u>? PBS NewsHour. [Online]
Available:
https://www.youtube.com/watch?v=oy2H9M85Jng

Garza, A. Cullors, P. Tometi. O. (2013). Black Lives
Matter. Social Movement. [Online] Available:
https://blacklivesmatter.com/

Johnson, U. (2018). Dr Umar Johnson discusses
Obama's presidency, Black People's worldwide
situation, Africa & more. The Breakfast Club Power
105.1. [Online] Available:
https://www.youtube.com/watch?v=hpkNsikbVuM
&t=349s

Jones, J. M. (1996). <u>Prejudice and Racism</u>. (2nd Ed.)
Columbus OH: McGraw-Hill

Keith, T. and Kelly, A. (2015). <u>Hillary Clinton's 3-Word
Misstep: 'All Lives Matter.</u>' NPR.ORG. [Online]
available:
https://www.npr.org/sections/itsallpolitics/2015/06/
24/417112956/hillary-clintons-three-word-gaffe-all-
lives-matter

McGuire, B. C. (2019). <u>The Ignoble Paradox of Man</u>. (Revised Ed.) Kindle Direct Publishing, Indie Publishing. [Online] Available: www.amazon.com

Mckesson, D. (2019). <u>Black Lives Matter Activist DeRay McKesson on Reparations for Slavery</u>. (Social Media). BBC Newsnight: https://www.youtube.com/watch?v=UAMhi96ru_Y

Ogbar, J. O. G. (2007). <u>Hip-Hop Revolution: The Culture and Politics of Rap</u>. Lawrence, Kansas. University Press of Kansas.

Rothman, R. A. (1999). <u>Inequality and Stratification: Race, Class, and Gender</u>. (3rd Ed.). Upper Saddle River, New Jersey. Prentice Hall

Sears, D. O. (1987). <u>Symbolic Racism</u>. In P. Kitz & D. Taylor (Eds.), Towards the Elimination of Racism: Profile in Controversy. New York: Plenum

Smiley, T. & West, C. (2012). <u>The Rich and the Rest of Us.</u> Carlsbad,California: SmilyBooks

Strategy Camp (2017). <u>Donald Trump is Unimpeachable. Here's Why</u>. [Online] Available: https://medium.com/siip-campaigns/donald-trump-is-unimpeachable-heres-why-f0a7db94d484

Terrell, K. (2016). Black Lives Matter Releases Policy Demands, Includes Reparations And Abolishing The Death Penalty. The Center for Popular Democracy. [Online] Available: https://populardemocracy.org/news-and-publications/black-lives-matter-releases-policy-demands-includes-reparations-and-abolishing

Trump D. J. (2019). Donald J. Trump and Collusion. Social Media [Online] Available: https://www.youtube.com/results?search_query=donald+j.+trump+and+collusion

Trump D. J. (2019). Donald Trump and the Road to the White House. Social Media [Online] Available: https://www.youtube.com/results?search_query=donald+trump+the+road+to+the+white+house+

West, C. (2008). Hope on a Tightrope. Carlsbad,California: SmilyBooks

West, C. (2017). Race Matters: Boston, Massachusetts: Beacon Press

www.ingramcontent.com/pod-product-compliance
Lightning Source LLC
Chambersburg PA
CBHW070655250726
48662CB00001B/132